Sea Glass Stories

Angela Welch Prusia

Sea Glass Stories
Copyright © 2023 by Angela Welch Prusia

This book is a work of fiction. Any references to historical events, real people or real locales are used fictitiously. Other names, characters, places and incidents are products of the author's imagination, and any resemblance to actual events or locales or persons, living or dead, is entirely coincidental.

All rights reserved. No part of this book may be reproduced or transmitted in any form or by any means without written permission from the author.

Summary: When Avery's parents decide to become foster parents, she's angry. No one asked her about a stranger living in her house and upending her life. Worse yet, CJ is joining the family vacation. But when life takes an unexpected twist, Avery is confronted with her own vulnerabilities. How will she respond to the foster girl she hates when the two share more in common than their differences?

Scripture quotation, as noted, come from this translation: *The Holy Bible, New International Version.* Copyright © 1973, 1978, 1984, 2011 by Biblica, Inc. Used by permission. All rights reserved worldwide.

Cover: Mercedes Piñera www.crowdspring.com
Contact the author: www.angelawelchprusia.com

ISBN: 9798872716280
Kindle: B0CQV64L53

Also by Angela Welch Prusia

———————————————

BRAiN RIDE

Late Summer Monarch

Tandem

Anonymous

Nameless

Faceless

Fearless

Headlock

Pinned

Match

For my girls.
A small tribute to you
when your lives got turned upside down.

Sea Glass Stories

CJ

I've scrolled enough data online to know the statistics by heart. My mind can't erase the charts and pie graphs plotting the awful facts.

An average of 106 people die in car accidents each day in America.

Drunk driving causes 1 in every 3 of these fatalities.

Every country has its own staggering records.

But cold statistics strip away the human side.

Hiding behind every number is a person.

A story.

Like the day my entire life turned inside out.

One minute I was sketching our dog Oscar, trying to capture the way his eyes can read the nuance of my every mood.

The next minute, Mom and I were speeding to the hospital, rushing into the ER where she crumpled to the floor at the horrible news.

The accident took both their lives.

I still hear the raw cry that erupted from the depths of my mother's very soul.

I could only stand there, numb, while my brain tried to comprehend the strange words coming from the doctor's mouth.

I'm so sorry. We tried to save them. But they're gone.

May 2. 1:09 p.m.

The fateful day time came to a jolting halt.

The day a 51-year-old woman with three DUIs stumbled out of a downtown bar and got into her 2005

Mazda Protegé. Two blocks away, this same woman ran a red light going 45 miles an hour and broadsided a 1971 candy apple red Ford Galaxie 500 driven by a 37-year-old male with a toddler in the back seat.

All the details are in the accident report.

The one I've read hundreds of times.

Every word haunts me.

I can't rewrite the facts.

No matter how hard I try, I can't undo the day that forever changed my life.

My father was the 37-year-old male. He died in the ambulance en route to the hospital. The last words on his lips expressed his love for my mom, me, and Toby.

Toby.

My little brother was strapped in his car seat in the back seat probably singing his lungs out to the *Wheels on the Bus*.

I used to hate his preschool playlist.

Now, I'd give anything to hear my little brother sing along to the music.

The wipers on the bus go back and forth. Back and forth.
The horn on the bus goes beep, beep, beep. Beep, beep, beep.
The driver on the bus says, "Move on back. Move on back."

Three-year-olds aren't supposed to die.

He would be finishing his kindergarten year.

Toby's sixth birthday is tomorrow.

I've already got my backpack loaded with spray paint. Skipping school is nonnegotiable.

The day is hard enough without having to endure my newest educational institution. I've been in five schools since the accident. The straight A honor roll student now scrapes by with Ds—except in art, the only thing keeping me sane.

I never skipped school before the accident.

Never broke the rules.

I was a model child.

Not the rebellious teenager who bounces from foster home to foster home. The runaway who can't outrun her heartache.

I ditched school for the first time three years ago.

On picture day.

Before Mom got admitted to the hospital.

For the first time.

Before foster care.

When I still lived at home for those few awful months after the accident. The only home I'd ever known. The white house with the window boxes on Magnolia Circle, the cul-de-sac two blocks from my elementary school.

The pictures lining the hall were too painful to see. I saw the progression of my photos from preschool until middle school, and it hit me hard.

Toby would never smile for a school picture again.

I would keep growing, but he was stuck in time. I couldn't bear the thought of Toby's last professional picture next to my ever-changing school pictures.

The one taken of him at preschool in his overalls in front of a backdrop of Crayola crayons. A smattering of freckles is splayed across his nose. The tuft of hair that sticks up in back used to bother my mom. Now the picture is just as treasured as my father's last gift to her—a silver necklace with each of our birthstones for their 15th wedding anniversary.

Three years have passed since that horrible day.

A day I want desperately to forget.

But can't.

Avery

Sea glass has fascinated me since the first time I saw the sunlight glint off a piece of cobalt blue glass wedged between a rock and a piece of driftwood on the shores of Puget Sound. I was probably 8 or 9 when we visited my grandparents at their new home in Bremerton, Washington. After 20 years in the Navy, they retired and returned to their first duty assignment, an area they fell in love with after being stationed there.

Looking for shells while my little sister played in the water with my dad, I saw the blue color out of the corner of my eye. I plucked the rounded glass the size of a penny from its resting spot and rubbed the frosted surface, marveling at its beauty.

"Did you find a piece of sea glass?" Grams clapped, excited for me.

I looked at her, squinting in the sunlight. "What's sea glass?"

"Trash turned treasure." My grandmother's hazel eyes sparkled under her straw hat. She explained how the ocean naturally heals itself by recycling discarded glass.

Her words drew me in like poetry.

"The ocean is nature's very own rock tumbler."

I gazed across the expanse of water, imagining broken fragments of glass tossed by the waves, tumbling against the abrasive salt and sand, much like the rock tumbler Papa had in his garage.

"The process can last decades." Grams rubbed the frosted piece between the pads of her fingers.

Apparently, cobalt, soft blue, cornflower, and aqua shades used in medicine bottles and decorative pieces are favorites for collectors, but less common than clear, brown, and green. Roughly 1 in 250 pieces are this beautiful blue color.

I was hooked.

Obsessed with sea glass.

I had to learn more.

Red, orange, and yellow sea glass are the ultimate treasure for beachcombers to find. For a long time, a colorant that used real gold was added to red and orange bottles, so only the wealthy could afford these fiery shades. The odds of finding a red piece is 1 in 5,000, and 1 in 10,000 for orange or yellow.

Fascinated, I kept scrolling online to research. I don't think I slept more than a couple hours that night in the guest room where I shared a queen bed with my little sister who snored, oblivious to the laptop screen illuminating the dark.

Sea glass has a frosted appearance due to a chemical transformation called hydration. The soda and lime used in the glass making process reacts with saltwater and causes pitting on the surface.

Each piece of glass has a story. In the past, dumping trash into the ocean was common, especially along shipping lanes and shorelines. Serious collectors love the hunt as much as discovering the origin of the piece, whether from a shipwreck or from another source.

Most sea glass started out as bottles—wine, beer, whiskey, perfume, soda, medicine, seltzer water, even cosmetic jars. However, other sources of glass include:

- Carnival glass. Flower vases, bowls and candy dishes made from pressed glass from 1905 into the 1930's have an iridescent shimmer.
- Bonfire glass. Any glass melted by a campfire or dump fire. More than one color of bottle may have melted together or may include trapped sand, water, or other small objects in the glass.
- Glass floats. Colorful aqua and green balls wrapped in rope and tied together to keep fishing nets afloat.
- Depression glass (crystal, pink, pale blue, green and amber) was distributed for free or low cost during the Great Depression.
- Milk or opaque glass (white, pink, yellow, blue and brown) originated in 16th century Venice and was mass produced in the 1950's and '60s.
- Multi-colored refuse glass. Leftover globs of glass from glass blowers honing their skills.
- Old light bulb insulators (often deep purple) or electric power and phone line insulators (usually teal).
- Bottle stoppers, jug handles, buttons, beads, and marbles. One site talked about the popularity of marble games in the past, including bored teenagers who would use marbles as ammo, aiming for dumpsters or rats.

Six years after my first find, I've found enough sea glass to fill over two dozen glass bottles. My room features my collection of nature's art.

Grams and I love to go thrifting where I scour the shelves to find unique glass jars to hold my finds. My favorite is an ornate bottle with a raised flower and leaf design which I keep on my dresser. Sea glass reaches the cork.

I'm landlocked where we live in the Midwest, so the beach is my happy place. Most of my sea glass collection comes from our annual summer vacation trips to Puget Sound to see Grams and Papa, though I'm proud of the small assortment of beach glass I found at Lake Erie when we paired a family trip with a work conference for my dad last year.

The terms sea glass and beach glass are often used interchangeably. They're equally valuable and beautiful, though technically beach glass is less frosty and pitted because it's found in freshwater lakes and rivers like the Great Lakes where countless shipwrecks have accounted for the large amount of glass—an estimated 6,000 according to a detailed map my dad bought for his office.

Between the wrecks and the garbage which was dumped into the lakes for decades until the Environmental Protection Agency got involved, beach glass is a little-known treasure that regularly washes up on the shores of the Great Lakes.

According to a jewelry maker I met at a cute little shop, the pieces found on Lake Erie are just as good as sea glass found along saltwater coasts. The beach glass charm bracelet dangling from my wrist is proof. Six small pieces of pale glass make up the charms.

I subconsciously touch a frosted green piece, my fingers rubbing the smooth surface, as my parents stand before me and my little sister. They called a family meeting. There is news to share.

Even Lola, our scruffy terrier mix we rescued from the humane society, wags her tail. She's sandwiched between me and Amiya on the couch, sensing something is up.

My sister thinks we're going to Disney World, but an ominous feeling washes over me.

The last time we had a little pow wow like this our dog had to be put down. Scout was my mom's dog from her college days, a faithful little cocker spaniel. Lola's still young, but that doesn't ease my nerves.

Something tells me life is about to change.

The look on their faces says it all.

What I've been dreading is no longer just talk. My parents are really going to do this thing.

I slump into the cushions.

My life won't be the same.

And no one even asked me.

CJ

I call it art.

But the probation officer says public property is not a canvas. Obviously, he doesn't appreciate Banksy, my inspiration and favorite anonymous graffiti artist.

The guy's a genius.

And gutsy.

Banksy drew international attention in 2005 with his image of a girl clutching balloons which he painted on the West Bank wall in Israel, part of the barrier to stop suicide bombers. His iconic images like the protester throwing a bouquet inspire me to make a difference through my art.

But Mr. Law Enforcement sees things differently.

I want to explain how complementary colors on the color wheel are found opposite each other. Why I chose yellow and purple, green and magenta spray paint to make my masterpiece.

He says I'm defacing public property.

Even when I flash my biggest smile and try to convince the kind policeman otherwise.

I didn't paint gang symbols or anything profane. I wanted to bring color to an otherwise drab wall. Enhance my community.

Mr. Law Enforcement just frowns.

I plead harder, explaining how the blank cement was calling my name, begging me to create. Bikers and runners use the trail that goes under the bridge. Keeping in shape is enough of a challenge. Who wants to stare at a boring cement wall? I wanted to give these dedicated souls a splash of color to inspire them as they got their sweat on.

But I can't convince him of the merits of my artwork.

Had I succeeded, I wouldn't have this monitor strapped to my leg. Which really sucks because it's chafing my skin. And cramping my style. One more infraction, and I'll land in juvenile detention.

Maybe my record will help my street cred as a graffiti artist. Banksy has taken risks that have contributed to his legendary status.

I dream of making the same impact with my art.

My favorite Banksy story was when he was painting graffiti on a train with some of his friends. He was just age 18 at the time when the police showed up. His friends escaped, but Banksy spent an hour hiding under a dumper truck with engine oil leaking all over him.

I can't even imagine.

But Banksy wasn't deterred.

As he lay there listening to the cops, inspiration hit. He stared up at the stenciled plate on the bottom of the fuel tank and realized stencils were his answer. They would cut his painting time in half, so he didn't have to give up his graffiti art.

When Banksy later cut out his first stencil, he told his friend he liked the political edge. That he could feel the power in the stencil. I wrote his quote across the cover of my sketch pad.

"All graffiti is low-level dissent, but stencils have an extra history. They've been used to start revolutions and to stop wars."

If only Mr. Law Enforcement were interested in a little art history, but he could care less about my graffiti hero.

No one ever asks me anything that matters. The real reason I skipped school today.

Who cares about another troubled teenager? An angry girl with a bad attitude.

No one even bothered to notice the artwork. It's my best graffiti work yet. A little boy in overalls with a balloon in one hand and a big red lollipop in the other.

It doesn't take a detective to look at a calendar and see the pattern. I don't just ditch school at random. I escape four days a year.

April 12, Toby's birthday.

May 2, the day of the accident.

August 9, the day I got put in foster care.

October 16, my dad's birthday.

Every day is a struggle, but the anniversary days—those are brutal. I wake up barely able to breathe. Escaping is how I survive.

The thought of Toby and my dad being forgotten makes me crazy, so I commemorate their lives with a little graffiti art on a concrete wall needing a splash of color.

In my book, that's not criminal.

But the people in charge of the screwed-up system see otherwise.

If I made the rules, I would welcome art. Color and beauty make everyone a little happier.

So, it's no surprise that the foster parents called the cops when I didn't show up after school. I lost track of time—one of the many reasons I love art. For just a moment, I'm in this space of forgetfulness, a place I don't have to remember.

When the police found me adding the final touch to my masterpiece, my fate was sealed.

Surprise, surprise. I got strapped with an ankle monitor, and my foster parents put in their two weeks' notice. They quit. The caseworker has 14 days to figure out where I live next.

I can see the fear in their eyes. They think I'm a criminal, a delinquent who will deface their cars and homes. They say I'm too much of a bad influence on their younger children. Babies are more their style. Not an unstable almost-14-year-old girl with hormones.

Let them believe the lies.

I'm not going to explain myself if they make assumptions. Don't foster parents receive some type of training that tells them to look behind the behaviors to the cause of the pain?

My caseworker is already making calls, trying to convince another unsuspecting family to give me a chance like I'm some animal at the humane society needing a home.

I need my sketchbook.

It's the only escape from my crappy life.

Avery

I don't do messy.

Even when I was a kid in preschool, fingerpainting repulsed me. Where other kids loved sticking their fingers into the cool globs of paint, staining their fingers in primary colors, I stood back.

"Just try." My teacher knelt in front of me, her face filled with anticipation. "It's fun."

But I backed up against the wall, thrusting my hands into my pockets. I had no desire to become the next Picasso.

My mom says something, drawing me out of my head and back to the family meeting. All I hear is the question.

"What do you think?" She lights up, waiting for my reaction.

"Think about what?"

"We got our first placement."

"Placement?"

Dad looks ready to burst. "We're officially foster parents. The caseworker called an hour ago to tell us about a girl your age who needs a home."

How can they be so excited about some random stranger invading our home? I don't do well with change, and I don't trust people unless I really know them. Like my best friend Lucia who I've known for 10 of my 14 years on the planet. I'm an introvert who needs her space to unwind.

My parents don't have answers to my questions. There's this shroud of privacy around kids in foster care—which doesn't help my nerves. What if the person coming to live with us is a thief or a pathological liar? Or some psycho with anger issues who hurts baby animals or wants to blow things up?

I didn't sign up for this.

The only thing the caseworker mentioned is the girl is some type of wannabe graffiti artist. Her last foster parents let her go when she got caught defacing public property.

The knot in the pit of my stomach grows. I like my quiet, predictable world. But our life is about to get real messy.

Literally and figuratively.

Talk about ironic.

Mom clasps her hands. "Isn't it exciting?"

More like terrifying.

Ever since my parents got it in their heads to become foster parents, I begged them to reconsider. They volunteer at this summer camp for at-risk teens where they meet a dozen youth in need of a safe family. When they signed up for foster care classes, I figured they would lose interest, but their passion has only increased. They've been counting down the days for a call.

I'm a sucker for a good sob story as much as the next guy, but that doesn't mean I want someone in my space 24/7. That's a lot to ask anyone, even the most saintly of souls.

"We can't say no, Avery." Mom's hazel eyes fill with tears as she makes her case. She's always had a tender heart. "The caseworker is desperate. She can't find a placement for the girl. Something about troubled teenagers scares most people, but we can't ignore the need. There are just too many kids needing a good home."

Of course, my little sister is doing a happy dance around the living room at the news. She's wanted a baby brother or sister for years.

I'm just fine with our family of four, but my parents say we have the space. Maybe they decided fostering was a good compromise over having another kid.

Whatever the motivation, I'm less than thrilled with the idea.

Lola joins Amiya's excitement, running around in circles and barking. I already have a headache, and the graffiti artist hasn't even made her appearance.

I try to argue, but my protests sound bad—even to me. Basically, everyone in my family is a nice human. I'm the selfish one.

"Just give her a chance," Dad adds. He doesn't say it, but a mentor made a difference in his teens when his dad lost his job. "Life's been rough. We want to give this young lady the same loving, stable home we provide to you and your sister."

I'm not convinced.

But I don't pay the bills.

So, my vote doesn't count.

Five minutes later, I collapse on my bed, not sure if I want to cry or scream. A dozen emotions collide inside me like an explosion of fireworks.

I don't know what to do, so I call Grams. My grandmother always listens, making me feel heard. When I ask if I can move in with her and Papa, she reminds me that summer is just around the corner. We'll see each other in a few weeks.

"Look at your sea glass collection and remember your happy place," Grams tells me. "That's what I do when I'm scared."

Of course, my grandmother would know exactly how I'm feeling—even if I never admitted my fear.

The unknown is terrifying.

CJ moved in 48 hours later.

CJ

I change schools more than my hair.

And that's a lot.

I hardly remember my natural color. For the last three years, I've experimented with pink, purple, green, bleach blonde and now black. I've gone from long to shoulder-length to half-shaved to completely buzzed. Currently my hair is spikey short. Who knows what will strike my fancy six months from now.

And lucky me, it's standardized test day.

I tried to get out of the testing since I'm moving foster homes and schools, but no one listens.

"Your new school will ask for your records," the counselor explained. "These measurements help us assess where you are."

She took my grunt as agreement.

I could care less what someone says about my intelligence or lack of brain matter.

The ovals on the answer page make my vision blurry from the lack of pattern and color.

I sharpen my pencil.

Time to hone my art skills.

I visualize the geometric patterns reminiscent of Greek art on pottery that flourished toward the end of the Greek Dark Ages. Much of the pottery comprised funeral vases holding the ashes of the deceased. So, it seems only fitting since I'm probably digging my own grave.

But seriously, why should I even try?

My caseworker told me to pack my things. I'm moving after school.

All my possessions fit in two black garbage bags.

Talk about a killer to your self-esteem.

In case I wasn't messed up enough, I get the subtle hint. *You're trash, kid.*

I darken another oval, digging the pencil into the paper hard enough to make it tear.

Life in foster care is slowly killing me.

Avery

I got the mom look when I gave CJ a fake smile, but this is not my project. Forty-eight hours is not enough time to prepare for the earthquake upending our lives.

The girl looks like trouble with her black fish net stockings, shorts, crop top and combat boots. Multiple piercings, heavy makeup and short spiked hair complete the look.

Her eyes shoot darts.

She hates the world, or at least me.

I feel trapped in my own house.

I never asked for this.

Mom and Dad want me to play nice, but I don't have to like that someone else is consuming the same oxygen in my house. Taking up residence in the guest bedroom across from my room. Sharing our bathroom. My sister is annoying enough with the toothpaste she leaves streaked in the sink. Or the hair she leaves in the bathtub. Now CJ will be competing for the same space. If she leaves her dirty underwear on the floor, I swear I'll lose it.

My parents think they'll make a difference.

But I have my doubts. It took a year to build trust with our rescue dog. And Lola was easy to love; she's pure cuteness.

CJ comes with a rap sheet.

I'm pretty sure she bites.

CJ

I put on a show because that's what they expect. A little extra makeup and an edgy outfit gets a reaction, so in every new home, every new school I play the game. It's always the same. No one bothers to look past the outside to see what's really inside.

Someday I'll explore this in my art.

Create a series of self-portraits, showing the ever-changing chameleon.

But not now.

The pain is just too raw.

And survival takes too much energy.

My new foster sister—Amy, Alison or Avery, whatever her name is—doesn't even give me a chance. Judgment drips from her pores. The irony: in my past life, we could've passed as sisters or cousins. Long hair, light brown eyes, thin frame. But like everyone else, the girl convicting me only sees the façade.

She's already decided I'm a charity case.

Damaged goods.

Her parents looked so hopeful when we were introduced, like we'll be the best of friends, but she can't hide the nonverbal cues. She wants nothing to do with me.

Which is fine with me.

I could care less about her.

She thinks she's so special. But she's just like all the other biological kids—the entitled ones who have no clue how quickly life can change.

How one minute you're one of them.

And the next minute, your dad and brother are gone, and your mom is hospitalized because she's drowning in the trauma.

What's that old saying my dad loved to quote?

Never judge a person until you've walked a mile in their shoes.

Let me unlace my combat boots. The ones I found at the military surplus store for $10.

I'll gladly let you walk this foster care road.

A journey I never asked to take.

At least they have a cute dog. I don't do cats or reptiles. My last foster home had two royal pythons (a.k.a. ball pythons). I don't care if the scaly things weren't venomous or that they are the smallest of the African constrictors. The pythons terrified me.

I get the ten-minute house tour, but the layout of the rooms blur together with my last five or six foster homes. I'm losing count.

Is the bathroom the first door on the right or the second on the left? The worst is getting disoriented if I wake up from night terrors. My heart is already racing. Not knowing where I am triggers a panic attack.

Then there are the rules.

Am I allowed to rummage through the pantry or the refrigerator or do I need permission? Can I sleep in on weekends or is there a list of chores to complete? Are the wifi and Netflix passwords off limits to me?

This is the first time I know my foster parents. Turns out we met this summer when they volunteered as counselors, but that was camp. Just because we had fun together for a week doesn't mean I want to join their perfect little family.

Not when a drunk driver destroyed mine.

Mike and Olivia mean well. They think they can make an impact in my pathetic life, but nothing will bring back my dad or my brother.

So, I play the game and smile when they show me my room. At least I don't have to share it with another unfortunate soul who ended up in foster care. The door also locks which saves me from moving furniture to block the door at night. I can put in my night light without anyone teasing me for being a baby. I have enough nightmares without pitch-black rooms.

"You can paint the walls this summer if you'd like," Olivia says. "Make it your own."

They know about my graffiti art. Is this some type of trick?

The odds of me staying here aren't high. My life comes with a revolving door. In one foster home. Out another foster home. In and out, in and out.

"We're so glad you're here." Olivia looks like she wants to hug me, but I stiffen. Thankfully, she takes the hint.

"Get comfortable." She turns to leave. "Our home is your home."

Home.

The word hits me hard.

Will I ever feel at home again?

Avery

"Why don't you two take Lola on a walk?" Mom says after supper, but it's not a suggestion. "Show CJ around the neighborhood. Maybe stop at the Kwik Shop for an ice cream bar."

I roll my eyes, not bothering to hide my disdain. First, I had to help move her crap upstairs. Now I'm supposed to be the welcoming committee? The Kwik Shop is something I do with my friends—not her.

Of course, as soon as Lola hears the "w" word, she heads for the door. The dog is too smart.

Two minutes later, we're outside, and CJ cusses me out, throwing F bombs like grenades. I glance back at the house, hoping my parents can hear. My mom hates potty mouth.

"Let's get this clear, Ms. Perfect. I'm not a charity case." She gets in my face. "I'll be here less than a month. Guaranteed."

"Really?" My eyes light up.

"Don't get so excited." CJ kicks a rock. "I know when I'm not wanted."

My mom would want me to apologize, but I can't help the relief that floods over me. This whole experiment in foster care may be over before it even starts.

CJ

The only good thing about my last foster home was the roof. Even though I shared a bedroom on the second story with another foster kid, the girl could sleep through a natural disaster. As soon as I heard her snoring, I could slip out of the window onto the roof.

The pitch wasn't steep and there was a perfect spot where I could lean against the dormer window. Most nights I would take out my sketchbook and prop a flashlight against the shingles. I don't know if it was the quiet or the view under the stars, but my creativity soared.

I try the window, grateful the latch works. I'm sure my caseworker warned Mike and Olivia that I'm a runner, but they're either naïve or unconcerned I'll escape.

I discovered the treehouse on my second night. It's tucked out of sight in a leafy oak tree, the perfect spot to get away. I'm guessing Mike built it for the girls when Avery was younger. He's a man's man, the involved father who adores his daughters.

Like my dad.

He would do anything for me and Toby.

My favorite were the elaborate forts we built out of blankets strung across the furniture. He'd crawl in the hideout with us and match our imaginations. Whether we were pirates on the high seas or castaways on a deserted island, hours would disappear until Mom would lift a corner of a blanket and hand over peanut butter sandwiches cut in triangles, baby carrots and Rice Krispies treats.

I'm also assuming Ms. Perfect has outgrown the treehouse. She's busy with track season and friends. If she climbs up the wooden planks, it's probably on rare occasions. But still, I wait until everyone is asleep, so I don't add another reason for her to hate me.

Lola lifts her head when she sees me slip outside but doesn't move. Apparently, the furry thing has already accepted me.

The sweet smell of the outdoors fills my lungs. Wooden steps creak when I make my way up the trunk. I duck my head to avoid the ceiling beams; the treehouse isn't very spacious.

Hundreds of stars peek through a window in the roof while a moonbeam illuminates the little house in the branches. It's perfect.

I settle in the corner and pull out my sketchbook. There is enough light, I don't need a flashlight. A good thing—I don't want to risk getting discovered. Avery hates me enough; she'll freak if she discovers I'm hiding out in her treehouse.

I get my love of art from my dad. He was a tattoo artist who dreamed of illustrating children's books one day. I loved visiting the small shop where he worked with one other artist. There's something mesmerizing about watching a tattoo take shape on a human canvas.

Two hours disappear before I notice the time. My first day at my new school is tomorrow. I should attempt to make a good impression, though the ankle monitor will draw stares. And falling asleep in class because I stayed up all night won't help me gain any brownie points.

With only a few weeks of school left, I really don't want to move again—even if I told Avery I'd be out of here in less than a month.

Avery

"I wish you went to my school," my little sister tells CJ even though she's only in kindergarten.

"Me, too," I mutter under my breath. At least the girl isn't dressed in her fish net stockings and combat boots. Maybe the all-black outfit is her invisible look. I don't recognize the indie band on her t-shirt.

Amiya lights up. "Maybe I can bring you for show and tell day."

I give a humph. CJ is something of an oddity. I bet Amiya's classmates would have lots of questions. But more attention for the foster girl is not advisable. She's already invaded our lives enough.

"That would be sweet." CJ smiles, and Amiya claps. My sister adores her new sister. Me—not so much.

I sink in my seat, hugging my backpack and stare out the window. School ends in a month. Who starts a new school in the last few weeks of the semester? Maybe CJ won't last long here either. Apparently, the girl has already been kicked out of two middle schools this year.

Lucia sends me a message. "So, do I get to meet the new sis?"

I frown. CJ and I will never be related. Adoption is out of the question. My best friend knows better.

"She's NOT my sis." I snap a picture of me scowling.

"Lighten up. She can't be that bad."

My mother is bad enough. She wants me to make CJ feel welcome. I don't need my friends siding with her, too.

I don't want a shadow.

Or a new friend.

Or another sibling. I already tolerate my younger sister.

Mom pulls up to the school, and I ditch CJ as soon as the SUV is out of sight. If CJ is nervous, she doesn't show it. She looks like some kind of freak with her spikey short hair and black lipstick. Someone else can be her tour guide. The school counselor gets paid to welcome new students. Not me.

I have two tests back-to-back and a lab in science, so I almost forget about my sidekick.

Until lunch.

Of course, the counselor made sure to schedule CJ's lunch with mine so she could have a friend.

Even I feel a twinge of guilt seeing CJ alone with her tray at the empty table in the corner. She looks pathetic.

"Is that her? I love her hair." Lucia follows my gaze. "She looks lonely."

The tough girl doesn't look so threatening by herself, but that's not my problem. I take a bite of my sandwich, trying to ignore the little voice inside me telling me to be nice.

Why does CJ bring out the worst in me? Grams said I was scared. Is fear of the unknown triggering me?

"I'm going to invite her to sit with us."

Of course, Lucia's the better one. The girl is the very definition of kindness. She has a blind cat and a three-legged dog because she wants to save what others prefer to ignore.

CJ joins us a minute later. We exchange cold looks, but Lucia launches into *20 Questions*, barely coming up for air in the interrogation.

"Who do you have for homeroom? Oh, I love Ms. Spielman. That sucks you have science lab before lunch. Is it true Mr. Spencer has a class tarantula named Tabitha? What do your initials stand for?"

CJ doesn't answer that one.

"What was your old school like? You've gone to how many schools in three years?"

I tune out, irritated.

Lucia and I were in the middle of discussing our weekend plans, and now she's inviting CJ to hang out with us.

First, I have to share my family.

And now I'm expected to share my friends, too.

Having a foster sister sucks.

CJ

I hate being the new girl.

It's even worse when there's one month of school left. Even Avery made a comment.

Why bother to go for less than 30 days?

It's the one thing we agree on.

Seriously, who does that?

Enroll a kid one month before classes get out for the summer. Every other normal person moves at the beginning of the school year or at the first of the semester.

But foster kids aren't considered normal.

We're broken.

Unwanted.

At least it beats the alternative. Daycare. It's a thing for teens in foster care. Especially if you're too young to work. No one trusts a foster kid to stay alone at the house when the parents are at work. There's too much havoc us rebels can create.

I stick in my earbuds, put the hoodie over my head and avoid all eye contact. My strategy works for the first three periods.

Fourth period is a disaster. The American history teacher who doubles as the cheer coach explodes into my personal space like the classic experiment with Coke and Mentos. The woman goes over the top to introduce me and insists that everyone make the new girl feel welcome.

Cheer Coach thinks she's being hospitable.

I barely hide my annoyance.

When I hear the snicker from the back of the room, I resist the urge to bolt out the door. Some chick with a fake tan and bleached hair doesn't want to play nice.

When our eyes meet, Bleach Job doesn't hide her smirk. "Welcome," she calls out for the benefit of Cheer Coach, then mouths one word to me. "Freak."

Good thing there's distance between us because I want to leap over the desks and punch her in the face. But then I hear my therapist in my head and take several deep breaths. If I don't get in a fight my first week, she promised to buy me Hot Cheetos and Mountain Dew—my weakness.

I'm not sure if bribery is good counsel, but it works.

The rest of the class takes a test, so Cheer Coach says I can play games on my phone. "We start a new unit tomorrow, so enjoy the break."

It's the only thing keeping me from hurting Bleach Job. As soon as the bell rings, I slip out of the room and merge into the sea of bodies.

Lunch is just as awful. Everyone has their little friend groups, so I pretend not to care and take a seat in the corner by myself.

Avery ignores me. Her friends do not.

I just want the torture to end.

But the first day only gets worse.

I'm headed to gym when my latest nemesis bumps into me in the hall between sixth and seventh periods. Every school comes with a new bully.

This is no accident.

"Watch out, Freak!"

Of course, Bleach Job blames me. Mean people aren't very original. She wants to hurt me, but I let the words roll off me.

"I see your brain cells are on overdrive." I snort. "It's too bad you have such a limited lexicon."

Her mouth contorts like she wants to make a comeback but again, the grey matter is already taxed.

"Freak, freak, freak," I mimic, taunting her with her own vocabulary.

Bleach Job clenches her fists, her temples throbbing.

Score one for the new girl.

She's too dumb to match my verbal wit.

I take a step back and turn, hoping I can still avoid a tardy. I really am trying to follow the rules.

But the bully is mad, and her claws come out.

"Don't walk away from me." She pushes me in the back. "We're not done."

No one touches me, so I can't ignore the threat. Even Hot Cheetos and Mountain Dew can't compete with my pride.

People don't walk all over me and get away with it. Being in the system has taught me to be a survivor.

I slowly turn around, my eyes narrowing.

My bully matches my stare. She dares me like the antagonist in a shootout in an old Western. Cue the tumbleweed which rolls across the dusty street. Two gunmen pull their pistols from their holsters. Who will be the first to shoot?

Only this isn't Hollywood.

I'm in a showdown in a middle school hallway.

A posse of friends surrounds Bleach Job, each nose upturned. I don't meet their impossible standards, so I'm branded a loser. Their faces blur with a dozen other mean girls.

Same story. Different school.

My lip curls into a wry smile. It's almost laughable—the one-dimensional character arc of a mean girl.

"What's so funny?!" Bleach Job narrows her eyes, and I imagine a cartoon character, steam puffing out of her cartoon ears. The image adds to my amusement.

The girl expects to intimidate me like the other 99% of people who cower before her. But the verbal darts and body language don't hit their target which only infuriates her.

"Nothing." I shrug. "I've met you before in another school. Maybe it was your twin."

Her face contorts. My sarcasm doesn't reach her brain cells, but she's offended, nonetheless.

Like other mean girls, she considers herself unique. The prima donna of the school.

I move three steps forward, piercing her personal bubble. A cloud of expensive perfume makes me want to gag.

"I don't do bullies." I cross my arms and call her bluff.

Her posse gasps. Their small minds form one collective thought. *How dare someone stand up to their queen bee?*

"Fight!" someone yells, and all movement in the hallway ceases. Every eye turns toward us, waiting for the show to begin.

I don't have anything to prove, except to underscore my message: you don't scare me.

So, I take another two steps, bumping her shoulder in a similar display of aggression. Her posse parts, leaving me space as I head for class.

I expect to leave Bleach Job dumbfounded, but she is quick to regain her composure. She will not be humiliated.

A quick thrust of her foot, and I'm down. Of course, she will deny this.

I spring to my feet and tackle her before she can erupt in laughter. Caught off guard, she collapses to the linoleum floor with a groan. We roll around like two wrestlers on a mat.

A tangle of hair and limbs blurs before me as I struggle to gain the upper hand. Sweat beads my skin. I can taste the dust.

The crowd goes wild. Somewhere in my subconscious I register all the noise and cat calls, but I'm focused on one thing: making the enemy pay.

I punch Bleach Job three times in the face before strong arms grab me from behind and yank me off her. My ragged breathing comes hard.

She cowers against a locker, blood dripping from an open gash on her cheek. Makeup won't cover the bruises on her face.

"In the office," a deep voice barks. "Now."

Not good. It's the assistant principal.

The scowl on his face should deter me from making a smart remark, but I'm already in trouble. Why not let a few curse words fly?

"Show's over," he calls to the crowd. "Get to class or face the consequences of being tardy.

Kids scatter, but not before one more glance at me. I'm the zoo animal, the exhibit on display.

Thirty minutes later, I get suspended for two weeks. The other girl heads to the hospital. The nurse is convinced she needs stitches.

Of course, I'm the criminal. No one believes Bleach Job provoked me. They refuse to listen when I say she tripped me.

Mike can't get away from meetings at work, and Olivia has two more teeth cleanings before she can leave the dental office, so I'm left on a chair outside the assistant principal's office.

I would take a nap, but trust issues make sleep difficult when I need to stay on guard. So, I waste the time by drawing on my flesh with a black Sharpie I keep tucked in my backpack. I complete an arm sleeve before someone arrives for the prisoner.

Olivia is dressed in her scrubs, loose hair trailing her ponytail when she rushes into the office.

"I'm sorry." She's out of breath. "I got here as soon as possible."

The secretary nods toward me. "Mr. Goertz will talk to you soon. He's in a meeting with a student."

"What happened?" Olivia approaches me. She's calm. The wrath will come later.

But worry lines her face. Olivia isn't a jaded foster mom with experience. She still believes the best about me.

At least for another few minutes. The assistant principal will no doubt educate Olivia on all my flaws. He'll explain why I need a new learning environment. Why I'm so troubled.

I want to give my side of the story, but Mr. Goertz opens his door and welcomes us into his office where I spend the next 30 minutes listening to his lies.

Olivia asks for another chance, in-school suspension instead of out of school, but her request is denied. The assistant principal won't budge—not with a rebel like me in his hallways.

Bleach Job has witnesses. People who feed the lie. I was the aggressor. The one who provoked the fight. I protest even though I'm not surprised at the outcome. A thick file of prior crimes seals my fate.

I don't have a chance.

So why even try?

On the way out of the school I trip the fire alarm. If they want a criminal, then bring out the handcuffs.

I'm your girl.

Avery

Public speaking terrifies me, so I'm practically hyperventilating when Mr. Bowers calls my name.

"Avery, you're up."

I've practiced my how-to speech so much, I can recite it by heart, but I still take my index cards up to the front. Trying to balance a container of Grams' chocolate chip cookies to share with my classmates and a poster that details the steps nearly sends me sprawling across the floor.

Thankfully I catch myself, but I can feel the red flood my face. I'm a wreck.

"You got this," Lucia encourages me from the second row. I manage a small smile as I turn to face the crowd. Feeling every eye on me is unnerving.

"Do you come home from school starving?" I blurt out the first line in my opening too fast. If I keep this rate up, I'll lose points for not meeting the three-minute requirement.

"Do you stand in front of the pantry disappointed with packaged snacks because you crave something homemade?" I force myself to take a deep breath. "I have the perfect solution to your dilemma. Chocolate chip cookies straight from my grandmother's kitchen."

I'm about to launch into the needed ingredients when the fire alarm goes off, making me jump. My notecards fly out of my hands and scatter at my feet.

Everyone is out of their seats, voices rising to match the screech blaring through the building. My heart sinks. If this is a drill, the timing couldn't be worse.

"Students, please file into the hallway in an orderly manner. We didn't have a drill scheduled for today, so let's take this seriously," Mr. Bowers directs. "Sorry, Avery. You can resume your speech after our return."

I resist the urge to scowl. I was hoping for a pass. A good grade for a valiant effort during a potential fire.

Lucia catches up with me as we merge into the stream of students in the hallway.

"Someone lucked out of giving her speech."

"Luck?" I raise my voice over the chaos. Bodies are pressed together, adding to my anxiety. "I wanted to be done. This just prolongs the torture."

Somebody jabs an elbow in my side. I crane my neck, trying to see the door. I just want to escape outside.

We pass the office when Lucia grabs my arm. "Isn't that your mom? What's she doing here?"

I heard rumors of a fight between CJ and one of our resident mean girls. Ashleigh broke my glazed pot in elementary art because she got mad that mine turned out better than hers. I wouldn't blame CJ for taking Ashleigh down from her self-appointed throne.

But if CJ is behind the fire alarm, that's a different level of criminal. Pulling the alarm is straight up delinquent. The girl already has an ankle monitor. Does she want to go to juvie?

The crowd streaming out of the school is too thick, and my mom is too far away for questions.

"How much do you want to bet my foster sister is behind this?

"Really?" Lucia's eyes widen. "But it's her first day."

The little criminal could care less.

CJ has no conscience.

CJ

The screech of the alarm echoes through the halls, sending students and staff scattering. Of course, teachers and staff are irritated, but students are slapping hands and cheering. Any excuse to disrupt the school day is cause for celebration.

The hallways become a tangle of bodies as the mass moves toward the doorways. I join the flow and let myself get carried away in the stream of bodies out the front door.

For just a minute, I think of disappearing. But Olivia is close behind me. She's no dummy. She knows I'm a flight risk.

Besides I should celebrate with a siesta.

It's tiring being a bad girl.

I'm pretty sure my stunt got me suspended for the rest of the school year. I didn't even last one full day. That's a new record even for me.

The fire trucks pull into the parking lot as we make our exit. I can't help but think of Toby. My brother became obsessed with fire trucks after his day care took a field trip to the fire station, and he got a red plastic fireman's hat. I can still see Toby rolling his metal fire truck through our house, puffing out his cheeks as he made a siren sound. I was annoyed at the time.

Now I long to hear the sound.

The weight of sorrow presses against my chest. I miss him so much.

Guilt pokes an ugly finger into my conscience. If Toby were still alive, my little stunt would be so confusing to his young mind. Seriously, what kind of role model would I be?

Toby deserves a better big sister than I am.

Not a screw up.

I shouldn't have pulled the alarm. I really need to deal with my anger issues so I can honor his memory better.

But all these churning emotions inside sometimes just get the better of me. Stuffing them doesn't work.

The ride home is quiet until we pull into the driveway. Olivia turns off the ignition and turns to me.

"Save yourself the lecture." I open the passenger side door. "I'll pack my bags."

Something between surprise and compassion fills Olivia's eyes. "You're not going anywhere."

"It's okay. You're a nice lady and all, but I know the drill. I'm sure the school has already called my caseworker."

"Wait. Can't we talk about this?"

I'm halfway out of the car, so I stick my head back inside the interior. "There's nothing to talk about. I know you're one of those save-the-world types but save yourself the energy. I'm not your little project."

If my words hurt, Olivia doesn't show any offense. "Give me five minutes."

I want to take a nap, but she's so calm about the whole thing, I owe her. Everyone else raises their voices and rants over my bad choices.

"Whatever." I get back into the car and listen.

"So, I'm new at this whole foster parent thing, but I get it." She turns in the driver's seat to face me. "You're the new kid. It's hard enough to make friends when you're not the foster kid. But my guess is you didn't go out of your way to start a fight today. Avery's had issues with Ashleigh over the years. The girl is a bully."

I almost applaud. She's right, but it's too late. What's done is done.

"I may be older than you, but I've had my run-ins of mean girls." I'm surprised when she tells me about getting bullied at school.

"Middle school was the worst."

I resist the urge to make a smart remark.

"We could appeal the decision about the fight, but the fire alarm stunt probably killed your chances."

I wince. "Yeah, that was stupid. I wasn't thinking."

"Obviously." Olivia laughs, and the sound makes me relax. Keeping my guard up 24/7 is exhausting.

I lean back against the seat. Talking to Olivia is easy. "I have anger issues."

"Welcome to the club."

I raise my eyebrows. "You, too?"

She nods. "My best friend died from cancer a week before we turned 13. We called each other twins because she shared the same birthday."

I exhale. My own pain makes hers equally raw. "I had no idea. I'm so sorry."

Her eyes get watery. "Take it from me. Anger will destroy you."

The silence settles around us, but neither of us move. Olivia is right. Anger is easier than the other feelings—the hurt, the pain, the loss. Waking up every morning to the empty reminder of the loss. Those feelings leave me feeling helpless and vulnerable. Exposed.

"I have an idea." Olivia suddenly straightens in the driver's seat and turns the ignition. "You up for a little crazy?"

I don't know what to say. The woman is full of surprises.

Avery

This isn't like my parents. I don't see them anywhere. I scan the hill surrounding the track for the tenth time, feeling the disappointment rise. They never miss one of my track meets.

Or a band concert.

Or any event in my life.

Ever.

I need to focus on the race. I'm in the next heat, but my mind goes to CJ. Why do I have the strange feeling she's behind the reason for my mom's absence?

"You're up," Coach breaks my thoughts. "Get your head in the game, Crawford."

Heat creeps up my neck. Getting called out doesn't help my nerves. I take my spot and get into position. I should be visualizing a win, but I'm picturing the opposite. I'm so going to bomb this race.

I barely hear the words coming from the announcer's mouth; my heart is thudding so loud.

The starting pistol sounds, and we're off.

Usually, I find my rhythm within the first few seconds, but today, I'm completely off. Sluggish. One after another of my competitors pass me.

I know my time is awful before I even cross the finish line. Usually, I'm duking it out for first place. Today I'm lucky I didn't come in last.

That's when I hear Dad's voice calling over the crowd. "Next time, Avery. It's just one race."

When I meet his eyes, I can't even manage a half-smile. I'm so disappointed in myself.

Amiya stands beside him, but Mom is still missing. There's no time for questions. I have another event, and Coach is not happy.

I can't afford to get distracted.

CJ

Olivia's enthusiasm is unsettling, but she just smiles as she backs out of the driveway. "Trust me. You'll love this surprise."

I try to get her to talk, but she won't reveal the mystery. We make a quick stop at the thrift store for old tennis shoes, long-sleeve shirts and cargo pants which only adds to my questions. By the time we head out of town and turn onto a gravel road in the country, I'm completely baffled. Maybe even a little afraid.

A mile later, a sign reads, "Mad Cow Paintball."

Olivia laughs when I give her a strange look.

"Have you ever been paintballing?"

I shake my head.

"It's a blast. And a great way to get rid of a little aggression and anger." Olivia jumps out of the car and tosses me the thrift store clothes. "Come on. It's fun."

Who is this woman? I should be on house arrest, grounded for weeks.

Fifteen minutes later, I'm dressed in my new old clothes as we listen to a safety briefing. Helmets on and hoppers loaded with paintballs, I trudge after Olivia to the target range, wondering if I'm dreaming. The woman is a beast.

This whole thing is surreal.

Olivia adjusts her goggles and grins. She looks like a wilderness woman wearing the camouflage hunting pants she found. "Ready to do this thing?"

The hiss of the CO_2 and the recoil of the paintball gun freaks me out at first, but once I get the hang of shooting, I have fun hitting the targets.

The ping of the metal cans.

The splatter of neon green paint.

The satisfaction of making a bull's eye.

It's been a long time since I've had so much fun.

We join a group playing *Capture the Flag* in an area reserved for the game. Adrenaline rushes through me as I make a dash for a barrier made from old tires and take shots at my opponents. I whoop when I hit a girl in the goggles. Paint splatter will make it hard to see.

"Cover me," one of my teammates yells as he takes off for the other team's flag.

I aim for the guy guarding the flag, but I'm out of paintballs, so I need to refill my hopper. The timing sucks. My teammate gets eliminated.

I'm the only one left on my team, so I make a valiant run for the flag even though the odds are against me. Sure enough, I get pelted repeatedly. A hit on my upper arm stings. I'll probably have a welt, but battle scars come with bragging rights.

Olivia's team wins the round.

"Having fun?"

My grin matches hers.

Two rounds later, sweat rolls down my face, and I'm covered in paint. I gulp water.

I could do this for hours, but Olivia says she needs to start supper.

"What do you think?" She asks as we head home, windows down and music playing.

"I think you need to give up your country music and play something classic like ACDC or Kiss." I don't mention they were my dad's favorite bands.

Olivia turns up the volume just to annoy me. "I meant about the paintballing."

"Oh, that?" I shrug. "It was okay, I guess."

She elbows me, knowing I'm giving her a hard time. I wouldn't be teasing Olivia if the paintballing didn't take the edge off the anger.

"So, the girl is hooked?"

"Can we go again tomorrow?"

Olivia's laughter fills the car.

Soon we're both singing along to Garth Brooks.

Me and country music?

I'd blame my delirium on a paintball shot to my head, but I was wearing a helmet. I must be high on happy endorphins.

The feeling is nice.

Avery

I'm tired and hungry, but I want answers. Even Dad is worried when Mom doesn't return his phone calls.

I drop my bags at the door and call out her name.

She emerges from the laundry room smiling until she sees me.

"Oh, Avery." Realization hits. "I'm so sorry. I completely forgot about your track meet."

She reeks of sweat. A smudge streaks her cheek.

"Is that paint?" My mind scrambles to fill in the pieces, but nothing adds up.

Mom touches her face. "I haven't had time to shower. I took CJ paintballing."

This little announcement is hard enough to swallow when the source of my trouble walks into the kitchen sipping a half-finished mango smoothie. I swear the girl taunts me just to make me miserable. Getting a smoothie with my mom—that's our thing.

I'm so done with this little venture into social services. Being a foster family is not some feel-good Disney movie, but the doorbell rings before I can say anything.

"I ordered pizza." Mom gives me a hug. "Will that make up for my forgetfulness?"

"I'm not hungry," I lie. Track meets always make me hungry.

Mom gives me a look, but I storm up to my room without a word. I'm too mad to eat.

If I got suspended from school, I'd be grounded from my phone and all things electronic.

But apparently, the rules are different when you're in foster care. So much for justice. The girl should be under house arrest. If an ankle monitor didn't stop her latest stunt, what's next?

The smell of pizza drifts up the stairs, making my stomach grumble. I refuse to join them even if I'm starving. Someone needs to take a stand in this family. I'm not getting sucked into CJ's drama.

Lola jumps onto the bed beside me and gives me dog kisses. I snuggle closer, wishing I didn't have a pile of homework.

My gaze lingers on my sea glass collection. Summer vacation is just around the corner. Will I survive the last three weeks of school? I need a vacation from my life. I need Grams.

Lola snores beside me. If I don't tackle my algebra, I'll be doing the same. I grab a pencil and narrow my eyes. Something feels off.

I scan my room, taking in the stuffed animals tucked on a beanbag in the corner, a small bookcase, the clothes which missed the hamper, my desk . . . what is it?

That's when I see the disruption of dust on the back edge of my desk, right next to a picture of Lucia and me at the lake.

My Peyton Manning bobble head doll is missing.

Dad gave me the souvenir of the legendary quarterback to commemorate our first Broncos game together. The thing always makes me smile when it bobbles back and forth.

My eyes narrow. Finally, I have evidence. I snap a picture with my phone. The dust outlines the empty spot like chalk around a body in a crime scene.

Our little foster child is a thief.

CJ

My stomach is in knots, so I excuse myself after one slice of pizza.

Tomorrow is the day of the accident.

My caseworker told Mike and Olivia the date is a trigger, but with the whole fire alarm fiasco, I'm guessing they forgot.

I put in my earbuds and slip out the back door. I turn up the volume, hoping to calm the storm brewing inside me.

I can't forget.

May 2 is the day my world stopped spinning.

Avery

I march across the hall and barge into the guest bedroom, but CJ is gone. I look out the window and see her pacing across the yard.

The girl looks like a caged animal.

I hurry down the stairs and out the back door. "Where'd you put it?"

She takes out the left earbud. "What're you talking about?"

Her little act only irritates me. "Don't play dumb."

"You're too uptight, girl." CJ puts back in the earbud.

Ignoring me only fuels my anger. "My bobble head is missing."

Her eyes shoot darts. "I may be a lot of things, but I'm not a thief."

I cross my hands and humph.

"I know you think you're better than me." CJ deadpans. "But don't fool yourself. We're not that different—me and you."

I clench my fists. We're nothing alike. I work hard to get good grades and do well in sports. I follow the rules and respect authority. If CJ wants to ruin her life with one bad decision after another, I'm not about to get caught in the crossfire.

Let the evidence pile up.

It's only a matter of time.

CJ will be gone from our lives for good.

CJ

I know this is a bad idea.

It's an hour after midnight.

But I'm already in deep caca.

And I can't sleep. I'm haunted by dreams of screeching tires, crunching metal and police tape.

I should write a note, explain myself to Mike and Olivia. Tell them I'll be home in a few hours.

But words are so inadequate.

I can barely hold myself together.

Borrowing Avery's bike isn't my smartest decision, but the cemetery is too far to walk.

What's a little more ammo in my file? The thing is my own personal scrapbook, highlighting all my best moments in foster care. I may not have many photos of my childhood, but the state never forgets to document my every mistake.

Now they can add stolen property to my crimes. Avery already thinks I stole her stupid bobble head. She'll lose it when she finds I took her bike. At this rate, I'll be wearing this stupid ankle monitor the rest of my life.

Of course, no one will ask where I went—not that I would volunteer the answer. They will assume the worst. No one will suspect the truth.

Going to the cemetery is non-negotiable.

When we buried my father and my little brother next to one another in the plot in Row E, I promised myself that I would never forget. I would keep their memory alive.

I crawl out of my bedroom window, so I don't trip the silent alarm on the basement door or alert the home security system cameras.

Riding through the empty streets magnifies the emptiness inside. My legs are sore by the time I leave Avery's bike near the wrought iron gate and slip through a break in the fence.

A full moon illuminates my path as I find their headstones.

Devoted husband, loving father, artist, friend.
Beloved son, little brother, gone too soon.

The coffin holding my brother was so small. The picture flashes through my mind, bringing the familiar ache.

Everyone with a DUI should be forced to attend the funeral of someone under five. Maybe then, drunk drivers would think twice before getting behind the wheel.

I sit on the ground between my father and brother. An owl hoots in the distance, reminding me of one of Toby's favorite books. *The Very Busy Spider* by Eric Carle.

Mom would ask me to read to him, but after the tenth time through the book, I'd get annoyed.

Now I recite the book from memory. The words echo around me in the quiet of the night.

I'd give anything to have my little brother crawl into my lap and rest his head against my shoulder. I'd read for hours without one complaint.

Time disappears as I sit there, talking out loud about anything and everything. There's so much my dad and brother have missed.

My eyes get heavy, but I'm not ready to leave, so I don't move. I fall asleep, waking when the first sun rays touch my face. For the briefest of moments, the warmth feels like Toby and Dad kiss each cheek.

I'm in that hazy sleepy place where I forget they are gone until my brain wakes up and remembers the ugly truth—my brother and dad are never coming back.

"I'll love you forever." I blow two kisses.

Condensation wets the bike seat.

I'm in so much trouble.

But it's Saturday, so maybe I'll sneak back inside before everybody wakes up.

I have one more stop to make before I head home.

Avery

Flashing blue lights outside my bedroom window wake me up. The clock on my nightstand reads four hours past midnight.

"I'm scared." Amiya opens my door and jumps on my bed. Her hair is matted on one side; she's holding a teddy bear whose right paw needs stitching. "Why are the police here?"

"The police?" I'm still groggy, so I nudge the blinds just enough to see my parents standing on the driveway talking to a police officer and his partner. I'm surprised Lola isn't going crazy.

"I think CJ is missing." Amiya whispers even though glass separates us from the scene. "She's not in her room."

Of course, the girl snuck out.

I can only imagine what the neighbors are thinking. Nothing exciting ever happens in our neighborhood in the suburbs.

Until now.

Our family will make the headlines.

I just want my quiet life back.

CJ

I'm not sure who put up the white crosses, but within days of the accident, a small memorial appeared on the scene. The first time I visited, the pain was so raw, I almost vomited. I left two roses and a plastic dinosaur for my brother.

An unseen force draws me here every year on the anniversary. Just like the cemetery.

My playlist is eclectic as my feet pedal without conscious thought from my brain. Toby's beloved preschool songs mix with my dad's favorite classic rock. Anyone listening to the songs pulsing through my earbuds would think I'd lost my mind.

Maybe I have.

My emotions are all over the place. Anger. Sadness. Grief. Fear. I'm a wreck.

A block away from the site of the accident I pass Marley's. Dad introduced me to white chocolate hot cocoa at the local coffee shop the day Toby was born.

I still remember seeing the first glimpse of my little brother. The tuft of hair peeking from under the blanket where a tiny body rested in my mother's arms.

"Come meet Toby." Mom motioned me to the hospital bed. "You are going to be the best of friends."

I crawled beside her and marveled at my brother's tiny fingers, the curve of his lip, the downy eyebrows. When she handed Toby to me, I vowed to be the best big sister in the world and watch out for him.

If only I could've protected him.

My heart thuds in my chest as I approach the intersection.

Mercifully, the third cross is across the street, tucked out of view. The public outcry over the loss of a toddler at the hands of a drunk was in the small-town newspaper for weeks.

I inhale sharply.

My gaze lands on the two white wooden crosses staked into the grass on the corner of Bancroft and Main Street, the taller one in memory of my father and the smaller cross for my brother.

The lone figure standing there is unmistakable.

My mother.

I hesitate, not sure if I should run to her or hide and let her grieve alone.

But the ache inside overwhelms me.

"Mom?" My voice sounds like a dog's chew toy.

"Clementine?" Her pupils dilate in surprise. The birthstone necklace Dad gave her catches the light.

I drop my bike on the sidewalk and crumple into her arms.

She stands like a mannequin. Stiff and unmoving.

The awkwardness leaves me reeling.

But just as I start to pull back, she relaxes and holds me tight. A dozen memories swirl between us, the painful ones buried by the embrace.

I can't remember the last time we hugged.

My dad and Toby aren't the only ones I lost the day of the accident. I miss my mother.

I don't want to let go.

Ever.

Avery

Thirty minutes later, the cops drive off. Amiya and I slip into the upstairs hallway so we can eavesdrop.

My parents keep their voices low, but we are directly above them, so we can hear most of what they discuss. CJ ran off. My mountain bike is missing—the Trek I spent a summer babysitting to buy.

I'm so done with this whole thing.

Amiya is halfway down the steps before I can stop her.

"I'm so sorry about the commotion." Mom gives us both hugs. "I'm sure the police lights woke you up. CJ ran off."

We follow my parents to the kitchen where Mom starts the coffee. Dad hates feeling helpless. He's going to look for her.

Of course, Amiya wants to come, but my mom shakes her head. "Go back to bed. We'll wake you up when we know more."

My dad heads for the garage and we head upstairs.

Amiya wants to sleep with me, and I'm too tired to argue. As my head hits the pillow, I'm out.

When she wakes me up five hours later, I jolt up, afraid I'm late to school.

"It's Saturday, silly." Amiya laughs. "I'm hungry."

My own stomach grumbles. It's almost one in the afternoon. "How about brunch? I'm in the mood for pancakes."

Amiya jumps up, clapping. "Can I help?"

The house is strangely quiet.

I'm guessing Dad didn't find CJ because her door is slightly ajar. My parents deserve a big breakfast after their long night. Surprising them with pancakes and scrambled eggs will be perfect.

"I want to crack the eggs." Amiya pulls the carton from the refrigerator. The kitchen will be a mess, but I can't convince her to watch cartoons; my little sister insists on helping.

Fifteen minutes later, the first pancakes beg to be eaten. We don't have to wake the parents. The aroma draws them. Everyone is in their flannels.

"This is nice." Mom adds hazelnut creamer to her coffee. "Thanks for making brunch. We all needed this."

"I had no idea we slept so long." Dad stabs a sausage link. "I'm starving."

Steam rises from the stack of pancakes I set on the table. Amiya drowns her pancakes in syrup. I add strawberries and whipped cream to mine.

Mom sets down her coffee. "When Dad didn't find CJ, we stayed up late discussing the whole situation."

I stop mid-bite.

"CJ is hurting." Mom looks at me with sad eyes. "Her behavior is shouting her pain. We can't give up, even though it's hard."

She may be empathetic.

I am not.

"Come on." My dad elbows me. "Let's just enjoy our Saturday. We have to take one day at a time."

When I don't respond, he grabs the can of whipped cream and points it at me. "Let me see that beautiful smile, or this is war."

I cross my arms, daring him.

Amiya gasps, her eyes widening.

"I warned you." Dad presses the nozzle, sending a string of whipped cream into the air.

Whipped cream splatters my face.

"Yum." I swipe my finger across my cheek and plop the dollop into my mouth.

Amiya grabs the can and defends me. Dad gets a handful in his hair. He shakes his head, letting the droplets fly.

Mom gets caught in the crossfire, but she just laughs at the whipped cream on her pjs. She's always a good sport.

I rush to the refrigerator for two more cans which we keep in stock because Dad loves whipped cream with his coffee.

"Here you go." I throw one of the sugary weapons to Mom, and she lets loose, spraying strands like silly string.

Lola starts barking, wanting in on the excitement. In seconds, whipped cream rains down on us. Dad wrestles the can from Amiya and sprays me.

I laugh when he runs out of ammo.

Dad dives under the table, followed by Mom. They try to form a human shield, but it's impossible to escape.

"We've got you now!" Amiya and I drop to our knees. Talk about an easy target. Burying their faces in their arms only protects their eyes. Everything else is exposed—the perfect target.

I don't hear the doorbell ring until my can rattles with nothing left. Amiya surrenders her empty can, and we all freeze, surveying the mess.

White fluff is everywhere. Whipped cream touches clothing, flesh, dog fur, breakfast dishes, even the ceiling fan above the kitchen table.

The doorbell rings again.

My parents crawl out from under the table like guilty children caught in mischief. They're covered in fluff when they answer the door.

It's the cops. They found CJ.

CJ

The cop driving me back to Olivia and Mike's house tells me I'm lucky. That I have a foster family who cares for me.

Lucky? Did you see the white crosses when you yanked me from my mother? Or saw the pitiful way her eyes followed me as I was forced into the back of the cop car?

I bite my tongue. I'm already in enough trouble. Disrespecting a law officer won't help my case.

Her partner says something, but I tune them out and slump in the seat. Toby would've loved the chance to ride in a cruiser. He'd be begging the cops to sound the siren.

We pull up next to a minivan at a stop light, and the kids in the back seat stare at me like a criminal. If only I'd worn a hoody; I could disappear in the folds of material.

I hate feeling so exposed.

Judged.

Look, it's the bad girl.

I'm so tired. I just want to sleep.

Avery

One of the police officers raises an eyebrow when he steps into the house with CJ. His partner bites her lip, trying not to crack a smile.

Neither asks about our whipped cream war or why we're covered in white. The kitchen is a disaster.

CJ looks exhausted. She snags a sausage link.

"I'm so glad you're safe." Mom is covered in fluff, but relief overshadows whatever embarrassment she may feel. "We were so worried."

CJ backs up when Mom tries to hug her.

"What?" Dad laughs, his glasses smeared in whipped cream. "You don't want to look as ridiculous as us?"

Lola barks, as if agreeing. Even the dog has flecks of whipped cream on her fur.

"Hungry?" Mom nudges the plate of pancakes forward.

CJ takes the whole plate. "Starving."

She inhales the stack, making Amiya giggle. My parents laugh and the cops join in. Even CJ manages a half-grin.

I'm the only one not smiling.

Once again, the foster kid gets off easy.

Where's the justice?

CJ

There's gotta be a catch. I stole Avery's bike. I stayed out all night. And the cops showed up.

So why aren't they kicking me out? I wolfed down the pancakes, sure that was my last meal for the day. Sometimes when I get put in emergency placement, I wait around an office all day. If I'm lucky, one of the caseworkers will get me some chips from the vending machine. But it's usually late by the time someone gets guilted into taking me, and food is an afterthought.

Maybe the whipped cream gave them a sugar rush, so they're not thinking straight. But Mike and Olivia insist they're not giving up on me. That I'm stuck with them.

"Our family stays together, even in the tough times." Mike gets a steely look in his eyes. "When I was a sophomore and my dad got laid off his job, we scoured trash cans to collect aluminum cans just to put gas in the car, but my family stuck it out together."

Olivia reaches for Mike's hand when his voice catches. "And we're stronger today because of the challenges."

Amiya cheers at the news; Avery presses her lips together in a tight line.

But her attitude is the least of my worries.

The cops give me a lecture.

And my probation officer is not happy. He's just mean enough to make my life miserable. His mission: get it through my thick skull that a life of crime is not for me.

Last time I checked, visiting the cemetery isn't a crime. But they've already decided I'm a criminal. I'm just another foster kid who will end up in jail or on the streets.

I hate my reputation.

Avery

Dad built a treehouse when I was in second grade that is still my favorite place on the planet. No matter how crazy everything gets, it's the one place I can escape. As soon as I climb up the wood planks which trail up the main trunk of the large oak tree, I'm in my own little world.

I don't know which season is my favorite.

Spring's woodsy smell of fuzzy new buds, songbirds darting back and forth building their hidden nests.

Summer's leafy branches holding me deep within the tree, cooling me from the sun overhead.

Fall's brilliance of color, falling leaves mesmerizing me with their fluttering dance to the ground.

Winter's silence, hundreds of stars glittering above, snowflakes falling around me.

I'm glad I grabbed a blanket to ward off the chill in the air. I hug my knees and pull the downy fabric around me.

The track meet thing still stings, especially when Mom took CJ out for paintballing and a smoothie. The little foster girl has upended our lives. Her world might be ruled by chaos and crazy, but my life has order and structure.

When did fire alarm stunts and police visits get rewarded? Did the rules change? Why does everything feel flipped like I'm stuck upside down on a roller coaster ride?

I feel invisible in my own house.

I pull out my phone and call Grams. As soon as I see her face on the screen, I can't help but cry.

"What's wrong, sweetie?" The wrinkles around my grandmother's face crease with her concern. Wisps of grey hair escape her ponytail.

Most of what I say comes out in hiccups and sniffles, but Grams listens like always and somehow deciphers what spills from my mouth.

"I wish I could hug you." Her voice is soft, soothing. "I hurt when you're hurting."

Another tear slips down my face at the tender words. Maybe it's just being heard, but Grams always knows what to say.

"I know you're disappointed, but you know that your mom didn't mean to miss your track meet, right?"

I nod, wiping my eyes on my sleeve.

"I'll never forget an essay written by a freshman in my first year of teaching."

I lean back against the cool planks and adjust the blanket. Grams taught for over 25 years. She has a story for everything.

"The girl wrote about missing the father she never met because he died in combat."

Grams gets a far-off look, and I wonder if she's picturing her student. She has a shelf of yearbooks from every year she taught high school English. When she retired, Grams estimated she'd taught 3,000 plus kids over the years.

"Amy—that was the girl's name—said it was the little things she longed for the most. Going out for ice cream and listening to dumb dad jokes or seeing her father in the stands when she had a band concert or a swim meet."

A grin tugs at my lips. My dad's jokes are the worst.

"Amy wrote how when her friends complained about their parents, she wanted to scream. She would've given anything to have one day with her father."

I puff my cheeks, letting out a deep breath.

"I'm guessing CJ can relate to Amy," Grams says without judgment. "Try to remember that on the tough days."

My grandmother is right, but that doesn't make sharing my parents any easier, especially when a crumpled piece of paper catches my eye.

CJ has been here.

"I'm here whenever you need to talk." Grams blows me a kiss before we hang up.

I get up to retrieve the sketch hiding behind an old tin box. Curiosity competes with my anger. I unfold the paper to see a half-drawn sketch of a little boy.

My eyebrows knit together. I expected skulls and demon creatures. Not a little kid.

Still, I frown.

Mom and Dad made it clear that CJ is staying with us no matter what she does.

So, I don't have a choice on the living arrangement.

But some things are sacred.

The treehouse is my space.

CJ

A crumpled drawing is on my pillow when I finish my shower. I sit on the bed, my wet hair wrapped in a towel. A note falls out when I unfold the sketch of Toby.

"The treehouse is off limits. Stay away."

My eyes narrow. I don't know what is worse—Avery's demand or her glimpse into my past.

I keep silent for a reason.

The pain is too raw.

But two can play this little game.

I'm not the only one with a past. I'm sure the family photo albums will have some great ammo to fire back at the girl who's become my nemesis.

Avery is going down.

Avery

My phone buzzes, jolting me awake 15 minutes before my alarm rings for school.

"Did you see this?" It's a message from Lucia.

A picture flashes across my screen.

Red creeps up my skin.

I'm staring at an awful picture of me from third grade. Mom snapped the photograph while I was sleeping with my reverse headgear.

The ugly metal contraption strapped around my head looks like an ancient torture device complete with a forehead pad and chin rest. I had to wear the horrible thing at night for a year to correct my underbite. Rubber bands connected an expander in my mouth to the frame. It fixed my underbite, but I don't want to relive the memory.

The phone rings. Lucia knows I need to talk.

"I don't understand," I stutter, remembering how Mom bribed me with ice cream when I threatened to rip up the picture. She insisted I would appreciate the photo when I got older.

A rush of dread hits. I can't go to school today. Not when the picture will be on everyone's social media feed. The humiliation will be awful.

How will I ever live this down?

I can already imagine the names.

Brace face. Metal mouth. Tinsel teeth. Magnet mouth.

I'll never get my first kiss.

Lucia breaks my thoughts. "Who would post this?"

My anger ignites. There's only one person to blame. My worst fear come true. My privacy violated.

I rush downstairs. CJ sits on a bar stool in the kitchen. Steam rises from a mug of coffee, a photo album beside her.

"How could you?" I hiss, pointing to her ankle monitor. "The criminal couldn't resist?"

She takes a bite out of her bagel, completely indifferent. I want to wring her neck. "You may have my parents fooled, but I don't trust you."

"Really, Princess?" CJ's eyes flash. "Is that why you've rolled out the red carpet?"

Her sarcasm grates on my nerves. "I never asked for this."

"Boo hoo," she mocks me. "I'm sorry to ruin your perfect life."

"Perfect?" I protest. "You know nothing about me."

"And you judge me every waking minute," CJ snaps. "A car accident destroyed my perfect life."

Her words make me stop. The sketch of the little boy fills my head.

She's said nothing about her past.

Until now.

"Don't sweat it." CJ jumps off the bar stool. "People will forget what I posted."

"Maybe in your world." I grit my teeth. "I don't have the luxury of moving schools."

Her lips tighten. "You think I want to move?"

I give a humph. "It's pretty clear you don't want to be here."

CJ crosses her arms. "I know when I'm not wanted."

I don't correct her.

"Exactly." CJ's face hardens.

I say nothing.

"People will forget about your stupid picture." She puts her coffee mug in the sink. "At least they won't forget about you."

CJ

I always get butterflies in my stomach before visits with my mom. We're supposed to meet once a week if the appointment doesn't get cancelled. My mom doesn't have reliable transportation, so I've learned not to hold my breath.

I haven't seen her since our chance encounter at the site of the accident. And that didn't end well.

Nothing like getting ripped out of my mom's arms by the police on the anniversary of the most traumatic day of my life.

After three years, you'd think I'd get used to the routine, but visits are so scripted, I feel like an actress playing another version of me. Lazy Saturdays at home in our pjs eating donuts just doesn't happen in a public setting.

As soon as the visitation worker pulls up in the car, my nerves kick into overdrive. I bite my nails.

The clipboard never helps, especially since I don't get to see the notes. We're the specimens under the microscope. A mother-daughter science experiment being studied, observed to determine if we can survive without killing each other.

Mostly we meet at the public library.

It's free.

And safe.

Mom's been in and out of homelessness since the accident. When she does have a place to stay, it's not always the best environment for a visit.

Then there's the string of loser boyfriends.

Thankfully I don't have anything to do with them. Seeing their pictures or hearing my mom mention them is enough.

I try not to wonder what my dad would think. I'm sure his heart would break seeing her like this. I know it kills me. That's why I get so nervous.

I hate seeing my mom so helpless.

She's so beautiful and so talented, but the accident left her broken. A shell of the mother I once knew.

The professionals say she has complicated grief. PGD. Prolonged Grief Disorder is when a person's extreme longing for the dead prevents them from carrying on with their daily lives. If functional impairment lasts longer than a year combined with other symptoms like identity disruption, intense sorrow and feeling like life is meaningless, the individual needs help to regain emotional balance.

When Mom lost her job after the accident and couldn't pay the bills, the school counselor got involved. Social services stepped in after a neighbor called. Her daughter was giving me food from their pantry on weekends when school breakfast and lunch weren't available. A caseworker came to the house for a well check. Mom got referred for help, and I entered the system.

I clutch my sketchbook. Doodling is the only way I survive our visits. That and card games. Keeping my hands busy spares my fingernails.

Once my caseworker Jillian asked to see my drawings. I was hesitant, but she's one of the nice ones—a big improvement over my first caseworker who cared more about her cigarette breaks.

Anyway, Jillian was impressed.

"They're just doodles." I shrugged, but she took the time to look at each one, turning the pages slowly and commenting on each one.

"You're good." Jillian looked me in the eye. "Let's talk with your foster mom about enrolling you in art classes."

"Really?" I couldn't believe it.

But my foster mom gave her two weeks' notice before Jillian could ask her. The woman was done dealing with me.

Today my mother is late, so I take a seat on one of the beanbags and find a fresh page. There's something about the white page that fuels my imagination. My mind's eye starts drawing before I even put pen to paper.

Twenty minutes later, I'm sketching a cat with big eyes and crazy fur when my mom arrives, smelling like coffee and lavender lotion.

The visitation worker notes something, but my mom doesn't make excuses for her tardiness. She showed up. That counts for something.

"This is for you." I hand her a sketch I drew of wildflowers along a fence. "Happy Mother's Day."

She tucks it into her oversized purse—a patchwork shoulder bag we found several years ago at the farmer's market, our regular haunt on weekends in the summer.

I take Phase 10 from my backpack. The card game is worn and missing at least one Wild card, but we don't notice. The game is our go-to on visits, something to play when the silence gets awkward.

While I deal us each 10 cards, I take in the sight of my mother. She's wearing a flowing skirt like normal. Long chestnut hair touches the middle of her back. To the casual observer, she looks like someone with a happy life. But I see the vacant eyes, the lines that etch her once flawless skin, the uneven fingernails she once kept polished.

"You can go first." I nod toward the pile of cards.

The visitation worker takes a seat not far from us, close enough to hear our conversation while still giving us the illusion of privacy. Once a friend from school joined me on a visit.

"Isn't it weird to have a stranger watching you?"

I shrugged. My life stopped being normal the moment I entered foster care.

"Did you eat breakfast?" I ask Mom, discarding a 12. She's so thin; I know she's not eating.

Mom can't remember, so I pull out an apple and a protein bar from my bag. It's so strange this reversal of roles—like I'm the parent and she's the child.

I nudge the food toward her. I wish my mom would eat, but she puts it in her bag. I can only hope she'll have an appetite later.

"I'm thinking about taking Spanish next year." I don't mention my suspension.

Mom surprises me when she spouts something off in Spanish. She spent two years in El Salvador in the Peace Corps before she and Dad got married.

"No comprendo," I say, remembering a phrase I heard on TV.

Mom gets a far-off look. "I could spend hours wandering around the outdoor markets, talking to the locals and bargaining for the best prices on mangos and bananas. The artist in you would be inspired by the colorful handmade fabrics."

I clear my throat, trying to mask my emotions. She never mentions my hobby. Probably because art is something me and my dad shared.

"Maybe I'll go someday."

Her smile reaches her eyes—something I rarely see anymore. My mother has been so broken since the accident; I stopped believing things could change.

But still, I can't help the flutter of hope beating inside my chest.

Avery

Summer vacation saves me. Everyone is too excited about the end of school, so my picture doesn't make the headlines.

Of course, there are a few haters. Ashleigh reposts the picture to all her followers. A mystery artist tapes a cartoon of a kid wearing headgear to my locker. And an annoying guy in science keeps calling me brace face under his breath. But it's nothing like I imagined.

I'm lucky.

Still, that doesn't erase what CJ did. I don't have to deal with her at school since she's suspended, but I keep my distance at home.

The feeling is mutual.

My mom gives up trying to make conversation at supper when the two of us give nothing more than one-word answers. Amiya has enough to say for all of us.

Before I can excuse myself, the parents want to talk about our upcoming vacation.

I can't wait.

Seven days without the foster girl.

I need a break from CJ.

CJ

This whole family dinner thing every night is not for me, but apparently, it's nonnegotiable for everyone living under the Crawford roof.

When they start talking about the family vacation, my temple throbs. Foster kids go to respite when the family goes on vacation. Been there, done that. Five times now, not that I'm counting.

The first family went to Disney and left me behind. I had my bags packed, ready by the door with the rest of the family's luggage, but they headed for the airport and my caseworker dropped me off at respite care. While the bio kids got Mickey Mouse ears and rode the rides, I got stuck at some old lady's house in the middle of nowhere. It was the last time I let myself cry.

I didn't even flinch when my next placement took their kids to the mountains. Or the grandparents who invited all the family (minus me) on a cruise to the Bahamas for their 50th anniversary.

Six Flags stung a little. The amusement park was only two hours down the road, and all my classmates had been there—except me.

That's the worst part.

I pretend like my life doesn't suck so I fit in with everyone else at school, but most of their experiences are things I only dream about.

"What do you think, CJ? Do you like the ocean?"

I don't realize Olivia has asked me a question until all eyes turn on me.

"Uh, I guess, uh, the ocean sounds cool. I've never been."

"She's going?!" Avery protests. The spoiled brat doesn't even pretend to like me, even though her parents are horrified by their daughter's response.

"Why wouldn't CJ go with us on vacation?" Mike is the first to recover.

"Because she's not part of the family." Avery grits her teeth. "Didn't the caseworker say something about respite?"

Olivia gives Avery the mom look. "We do not treat people with disrespect in this house."

Avery storms off, leaving an awkward silence in her wake.

"I'm sorry," Olivia sighs. "She's not herself lately."

I have my doubts, but I keep quiet, twirling my spaghetti noodles onto my fork. My grandmother taught me to use a spoon, but apparently that's not the way spaghetti is eaten here. They break their noodles in half before boiling them, so they're shorter.

That's something else you learn in foster care—trying to figure out how things are done at every new placement. Everyone knows the unwritten rules except for me.

"I'm not trying to excuse her behavior, but Avery's whole world has been turned upside down."

I bite my tongue. *And mine hasn't?*

If only I could live with my grandmother, but she's in an assisted living facility because of her dementia. My other grandparents are deceased which leaves my only other living relative—an unmarried uncle who has no clue what to do with a teenage girl.

I head to my room, glad to have my own space for once. Olivia let me choose the black comforter and teal sheets. The Disney princess bedding at my last place made me cringe.

I squeeze my eyes tight until the familiar sting subsides. I want my dog. But Oscar got taken away, too.

Sometimes I think my heart will burst.

Avery

What happened to family meetings?

Mom and Dad could've at least warned me before springing the news on me at supper. There's been no discussion.

Not that knowing early would've changed anything. I'm expected to plaster a smile on my face and be grateful for my good life and share with the less fortunate—no questions asked.

But the whole thing sucks.

Grams and Papa go with us on family vacations, and we only see them once or twice a year, so it's our time together.

So, excuse me for being a little selfish. I just want a break from the rebel child.

I'd call Lucia, but she'll call me out for being a horrible human.

And I just can't do empathy and nice right now. I want to rant and scream and throw my little pity party without guilt.

Mom knocks on the door.

"You want to talk?" She sits beside me on the bed.

Not really, but I don't have a choice. One of my parents' rules: we don't let the sun go down on our anger. We talk things out.

"I know you're not happy." Mom shifts her body so I can lean my head on her shoulder. "But CJ's caseworker said a vacation would be a good change for her."

I exhale. We're not rich, but my parents work hard so we can do something special every year.

"She's had a rough life, Avery. We want to give her a few good memories."

I sigh, knowing Mom's right—and hating it. I really am a nice person. CJ just brings out my bad side.

"Tell me what you're feeling."

"What's the point?" I snuggle under my comforter. "She's still coming with us on vacation."

"Because talking helps us process our feelings." Mom pats my arm. "We need to work through this."

"Fine." I let out a long sigh. "You missed my track meet because of CJ. And you took her out for smoothies. That's our thing."

Mom doesn't say anything, just lets me rant.

"Then there's the irritating stuff. Like flooding the bathroom floor because she doesn't tuck in the shower curtain. Or how she throws a fit if she doesn't ride shotgun."

"You have every right to get upset." Mom validates my feelings like we learned in our one and only family counseling session. The session that was supposed to prepare us for the complete upheaval of our entire life.

"I'm not in the mood for a therapy session."

"Fair but hear me out." Mom strokes my hair. "I can't give details, but there's a reason CJ prefers shotgun."

Of course. The girl can invade my life, but everything's private when it comes to her. CJ is a ward of the state. Mom can't even post a family picture online without covering CJ's face.

"She doesn't feel safe in the back of a car." Mom's voice catches. "Being there triggers bad memories from her last foster home."

I'm still mad, so it takes me a full minute to understand. The sudden silence reminds me how quiet the neighborhood is at this hour. An owl hoots in the distance.

"Oh." Guilt creeps into my consciousness. Now I feel awful. "I never thought about that."

"Me neither." Mom wipes a tear from her eye. "I never had to deal with all the stuff CJ carries. It's like our worlds spin in different universes."

Maybe, but what am I supposed to do?

Mom squeezes my hand. "Just give her a chance. That's all I'm asking. Try to look past the behavior."

I don't make any promises.

Mom gives me a hug. "Having CJ in our home doesn't change how much I love you. You know that, right?"

I shrug. My head knows this, but my heart has taken a beating. The reminder is nice.

Having a foster sister is a lot.

CJ

I pull out the worn photo I keep in my back pocket. The last one taken of my family before the accident changed everything. One of those random shots someone took when none of us was posing, and yet perfect, capturing the love we shared.

Dad wearing his favorite Braves hat, his arm draped across my mother. They were high school sweethearts who never left the honeymoon stage.

Mom wearing a straw hat and sundress. She's holding my little brother on her lap, his cheeks sticky from a red lollipop. And me, leaned against my dad, laughing at Oscar who's licking Toby's treat.

This whole vacation thing kind of threw me.

I'm torn. Excited, but nervous.

Going on a trip with another family feels weird. I should be traveling with my own family.

But that's impossible.

So, I'm not exactly sure what to feel.

Avery

My parents have some errands to run before we head out tomorrow, so me and CJ are supposed to clean the house and watch Amiya.

Neither of us are thrilled.

"Be nice to each other." Mom eyes us before waving goodbye. "I don't want to come home to a war zone."

"Then perhaps you shouldn't leave."

My mom laughs, but CJ isn't joking.

I grit my teeth. It's one thing we can agree on.

The door barely closes, and CJ takes off. "See ya, loser."

I block the stairs. "You have toilet duty."

"Whatever," she snorts.

"I cleaned the toilets last week. You're it."

CJ rolls her eyes, but I'm not backing down. "If we work together, it won't take long."

I wait for a fight, but she takes the toilet brush. I tackle the vacuuming. Even Amiya helps with the dusting when I bribe her with lemon drops.

The faster we clean, the faster I can binge on Netflix.

Mom drills me to vacuum thoroughly—back and forth, back and forth—but I cut corners and finish in half the time. I'm folding laundry when I hear something shatter from the living room.

I drop a pair of socks to investigate and freeze.

A glass vase is shattered at Amiya's feet.

Her dust cloth lays crumpled on the floor.

My little sister clutches her throat.

She's beet red, her eyes bugged out in sheer terror. *Amiya can't breathe.*

"She's choking." CJ rushes into the room and says what my brain is thinking.

But fear paralyzes me.

I can't move.

One thought terrorizes me. *What if Amiya dies?*

CJ crosses the room in one stride. She grabs my sister from behind and gives several sharp abdominal thrusts.

The lemon drop flies out of Amiya's mouth.

My sister gulps in air.

She collapses on the couch and starts to cry.

Everything happens so fast.

My own knees buckle as I rush toward Amiya. She falls into my arms, burying her face against me. I hold her tight for several minutes as my tears slip into her hair.

I can't bear to think of the alternative.

What might have happened *if* . . .

I would never have forgiven myself.

I look at CJ for the first time. She's pale, obviously shaken.

"If you weren't here . . ."

CJ cuts me off before I can say the awful words. "If I wasn't here, you would've done what I did."

I froze. I'll have nightmares for years.

I hug Amiya tighter and whisper a prayer of gratitude.

My sister is alive.

CJ

I slip upstairs, leaving Avery and Amiya to themselves. They need some sister time, and I need a shower.

Cleaning toilets is just disgusting, but now I'm pitted out, too. The whole choking thing left me drenched in sweat.

I'm just glad Amiya is okay.

I don't wish the loss of a little sibling on anyone.

Even my worst enemy.

Avery

I'm too shaken to pack, so I lay back on my bed and stare at the ceiling, my thoughts swirling.

The terror in Amiya's eyes haunt me. Guilt overwhelms me. I hate myself for my paralysis.

What if CJ wasn't here?

Suddenly the girl I've spent the last month hating spared me from an outcome I can barely let my mind consider.

If my little sister died, I would never forgive myself.

I turn to the wall and let the tears come.

The garage door opens. I need to tell my parents what happened, but when I roll over, something catches my eye.

My missing bobble head is wedged under my desk, out of normal sight.

CJ was right. She's not a thief.

CJ

Maybe I should've asked more questions. I assumed we were road tripping across country by car.

Not an airplane.

I never considered we'd be flying, or I would've run off again. I prefer the ground.

But Mike is persuasive, and he gave me this whole pep talk on how courage is not the absence of fear, but the triumph over it. I'm pretty sure he quoted Nelson Mandela which was brilliant. I've been a fan of the anti-apartheid activist and politician since I wrote a report on him in sixth grade.

Olivia gave me medicine for motion sickness just in case. And Amiya handed me a stick of gum.

"It'll help your ears during take-off and landing."

She hasn't let go of my hand through the entire terminal except when we had to go through security. Amiya has flown four times in her short life, so she's appointed herself as my personal attendant like I'm an unaccompanied minor. It's too cute to be annoying.

"We need to request airplane wings since it's your first flight," Mike says when we take a seat at our gate.

I protest. I'm not a kid.

Amiya shows me the one clipped to the strap on her backpack. "You can get one like me."

Thirty minutes later, Mike asks the flight attendant for the plastic wings when we board.

I'm secretly pleased. Even if they're cheesy, I want proof that I earned my wings.

I tighten my seat belt and clutch the arm rest as the attendants talk about oxygen masks and possible water evacuation.

"Standard safety briefing." Olivia pats my hand. "We'll be there in no time. Safe and sound."

I'm sandwiched between her and Amiya who pulls out her iPad. I wish I could be as calm and unaffected. The girl is a pro.

Mike leans forward to get my attention. He's sitting next to Avery in the aisle seat across from us. "Why do ducks need tail feathers?"

"Why?" I play along, knowing he's using dumb dad jokes to distract me.

"To cover their butt quacks."

The punch line is so stupid, it's funny—which only encourages Mike. The guy fires off a half dozen more equally bad jokes.

"What happens when a piano falls down a mine shaft? *You get A Flat Minor.*"

"How do you make a tissue dance? *Put a little boogie in it.*"

At the very least, Mike is entertaining himself.

And humor helps.

We're taking off down the runway.

My armpits are drenched, but I haven't succumbed to a panic attack.

Avery

The beach is my happy place.

As soon as we turn onto the one-way blacktop road lined with towering moss-covered evergreens and ferns, my heart quickens. If I was driving, I'd have a hard time obeying the hand carved wooden signs posting the speed limit—12.5 mph.

"Almost there. The Airbnb is just ahead." My dad rolls down the windows and gulps in the moist earthy air. "Ah, the Pacific Northwest."

I lean forward in my seat, craning my neck to see the first glimpse of water through the trees. As soon as the blue meets my gaze, I can't help the squeal that escapes my lips. My inner child is a beach bum.

"In case you didn't notice, Avery loves the ocean," my mom tells CJ who stares out of the window. The girl has never been out of the Midwest, so I'm guessing she's equally spellbound.

We pull into the driveway, and I leap out of the rental. Grams and Papa greet us with hugs. My grandmother feels extra thin, but I'm too excited about the beach to think much of it. While the adults talk, I throw my bag in the loft then head for the water. I don't want to waste one minute in my search for sea glass.

Everyone else is getting settled in the Airbnb. My dad found the place three years ago, and it's become a family favorite with its huge bay windows and gorgeous view.

Inhaling the fresh air, I take a minute to take in the site before tackling my mission. My grandfather once explained that Puget Sound is an estuary which is a semi-enclosed body of water in which salt water from the Pacific Ocean mixes with freshwater runoff.

The blue skies reveal majestic Mt. Rainier and Seattle's skyline in the distance. If I squint, I can make out the distinct shape of the Space Needle, remembering how my grandparents once took us to dinner in the revolving restaurant near the top.

I was about Amiya's age when the waiter brought out the Lunar Orbiter. The dessert is a basic sundae with vanilla ice cream and chocolate sauce, but dry ice bubbles and smokes like something from space. My mom snapped a picture of me trying to catch the swirling smoke around me.

Amiya has been begging to go ever since, so maybe we'll take a day trip to Seattle. Going to Pike Place Market and watching the fishmongers throw fish is quite entertaining. How they catch those big slippery fish always amazes me.

I weave in and out of the driftwood which has washed ashore. If I wasn't so obsessed with sea glass, I'd probably bring home a suitcase full of driftwood. The unique shapes are like sculptures straight from nature's art gallery.

Like usual, I lose track of time. Wet sand slips through my water shoes as I walk along the shore. The ever-changing shoreline adds to the adventure. Every wave brings new debris, making the hunt an adventure like no other. Hours feel like minutes when I get in my zone.

"I knew I'd find you here," Grams' voice reaches my ears.

I look up and smile at her approach. Her long grey-white hair is pulled into a ponytail. A loose cotton shirt billows in the breeze. Sandals and striped capris complete her outfit.

"Find any good sea glass yet?"

I uncurl my fingers to reveal a half dozen clear pieces. "Not yet."

She holds out a hand dotted with age spots. "I found a piece you might like."

A smile lights her eyes when I examine a beautiful aqua piece. The sun glints against the pale surface.

"I figured you'd like that one." She lets me keep it. "Papa and I took a short walk on the beach before you got here. Even 45 minutes in the car makes his back get stiff."

Thinking about my grandparents aging makes me sad. They've always acted younger than their 70 years, but I can see the changes. Grams is thinner, frailer, and Papa moves slower every year. He injured his back in the Navy years ago, but he refuses to use a walker.

I push the thought out of my head, and we walk in silence, the two of us bent over the sand as the waves roll into shore, the sound soothing.

"I met CJ." Grams stands to stretch. "When Papa teased her about her piercings, she held her own and gave him a hard time about all his ink."

I laugh. My grandfather is a big teddy bear covered in nautical tattoos from his time in the Navy. My favorite is the old treasure map on his right forearm. Papa had the tattoo artist weave each of the names of his four grandchildren into the cardinal directions on the compass rose.

"I like her," Grams says. "There's a sweet kid under all that hurt."

I'm not surprised by her comments. My grandmother sees the best in everyone.

"How about you?" she asks casually. "How are you doing with having a foster sister?"

I purse my lips together. "It's complicated." My feelings are so conflicted since CJ saved Amiya. I need to thank her, but I haven't found the right time.

Grams tries to meet my gaze, but I won't make eye contact as I return to my search for sea glass.

"Is it really that bad?"

I don't know where to begin, so I rub my fingers over a frosted green piece half buried in the sand. So much has happened. The fire alarm, the track meet, the cops, the social media post, Amiya choking, the bobble head.

Grams searches a pile of rocks next to a piece of driftwood. "Look," she exclaims.

I gasp at a beautiful, curved piece of cobalt blue.

"It's yours." Grams examines what looks like part of the mouth of a bottle before handing the treasure to me.

"I wonder how old it is?" I rub my finger along the curve, admiring the smooth surface.

"If only the glass could talk." Grams' eyes twinkle. "I can only imagine the stories we'd learn."

"Maybe," I begin our little game. "Two forbidden lovers enjoyed a bottle of wine before he proposed, defying the wishes of their parents."

"Or the glass was a rare perfume bottle belonging to a princess. An enemy slipped into the castle and shattered the bottle, threatening her life with a piece of the glass until the king's son saved her life."

Our tales always take on a life of their own.

"What if the bottle contained medicine that saved a young boy from a mysterious sickness?"

"And he grew up to become a doctor." Grams continues the story, the wrinkles around her eyes dancing. "And he saved an entire village from an outbreak, just in time to spare his one true love."

A giggle escapes my lips. We could go for hours, lost in creativity.

Grams threads her arm through mine. "You know, we're all kind of like sea glass. We each have a story to uncover."

The former English teacher can't forget her years in the classroom. Grams sees character arcs and plot lines in everything.

We walk closer to the water, so the waves swirl around our ankles before receding. Goosebumps rise to my flesh.

"Even CJ." Grams pauses, her face searching mine. "If you give her a chance, you might discover a story you never imagined."

The sun is sinking, frosting the sky in reds and oranges. The rarer colors of sea glass.

Leave it to Grams to see life differently. It's one of the most enduring things about her. Of course, she would see a metaphor in the broken glass.

Trash turned treasure.

A story waiting to be told.

Grams may be right, but CJ is far from polished. Her sharp edges hurt.

CJ

I could stay out on the wraparound deck all night with my sketchbook. The water's nice—from a distance. I don't swim, so the wet stuff scares me.

The rest of the family wandered down to the shore after dinner. Mike grilled BBQ chicken, pineapple and corn on the cob, so the scent lingers in the air.

The colors of the sunset spread across the water, igniting my need to create. I wish I had some pastels or watercolors to capture the scene.

An hour later, the last rays of the sun disappear below the horizon. A string of lights hung on the rafters illuminates my sketch. I usually draw people or animals, but my first landscape isn't bad. Gnarled driftwood in the foreground, waves lapping against the shore, evergreens ringing the bay, Mt. Rainier rising in the background. Maybe I'll even frame this one.

Flames dance on the beach where Mike stokes a fire in a metal ring. Goosebumps prickle my skin from the chill in the air.

I close my sketchbook and head inside. Grams is in the kitchen preparing a tray of s'more fixings.

"Come join us." She grabs the tray. "The night's perfect."

"I think I'll shower and head to bed." I yawn. "The two-hour time difference is hitting me."

"You can't miss s'mores." Papa emerges from the pantry with a half dozen metal skewers, a huge grin on his face.

I'm not about to argue with the elderly, so I grab one of the throw blankets and follow the two outside. The rest of the family is seated on plastic beach chairs around the fire, so I pull one from the deck and sit by Amiya.

The flames highlight her sunburned cheeks as she shows me a bucket of shells she found. Her favorite is a spiral with a natural hole.

"I'm going to make a necklace." Her eyes sparkle as she hands me a peach-colored scallop with a small hole in the hinge. "Grams brought some jewelry cord. You can make one, too."

"I'd like that," I say.

"Anyone ready for a skewer?" Papa hands out the wire sticks. "The fire's perfect."

"One or two?" Avery thrusts the bag of marshmallows toward me. Maybe she's thawing.

I pluck my marshmallow into the fire, careful not to burn my dessert. Amiya chars hers. The rolling waves sing a melody while the stars dot the sky like something out of an art gallery.

Seeing the faces highlighted by the flames stirs similar memories from the past. Sadness washes over me.

Mike is entertaining us with a story which only adds to my homesickness. I can't help but think of my dad. His random observations of life made me laugh one minute and cry the next. The artist in him looked at the world through a lens most people don't take the time to see.

"You're quiet," Olivia observes, nudging my leg. "Everything okay?"

"I'm just tired," I lie, burying my toes in the sand. "I should head to bed."

My therapist would want me to share my feelings, but if I start, the emotional mess will rush out in a torrential flood. And I don't know what to do with that.

Olivia reaches over to hug me goodnight and kisses my forehead. I hold back tears. My mom used to kiss me like that every night before bed.

"Goodnight," everyone calls out as I walk back toward the Airbnb. Every step feels like a stab in the heart.

I'm on vacation. I should be happy, right?

I survived my first flight. Being on Puget Sound is nice. And enjoying s'mores is always fun.

And yet, my heart is heavy.

Will I ever stop missing them?
Will I ever be able to escape the pain?

Avery

CJ is asleep in the twin bed across from me in the loft. The girl barely made it through s'mores. She's been out for an hour.

Amiya is curled up in a ball in a sleeping bag at my feet, but I'm too wired. CJ's night light doesn't help, so I slip outside and make my way to the beach. A full moon shimmers on the water while stars sparkle like clear sea glass against a black sandy sky. With the light on my phone, the night is perfect for searching for sea glass treasure.

Waves roll into shore, lulling me into my zone while I comb the beach. Peace settles over me. I could be out here all night.

My first find is a green piece of glass that looks like a mitten. I trace the thumb, marveling at the unique shape. I forgot to bring a container, so I tuck the glass into my palm, the surface cool against my flesh.

When my light catches another piece of glass among the sand, I hold my breath, anticipating the find. It's clear, along with the next several pieces of frosted glass. They're nice specimens, just not as exciting as the colors I treasure.

A few sharp pieces need to be tossed back in the ocean for further polishing, so I lob them into the water, but they don't skip like rocks. Hopefully the shards will get swept up and churn in the waves for months, even years. I like to imagine they will emerge again on the sand as perfect little masterpieces for the next sea glass enthusiast.

My back is stiff, so I stretch my muscles, careful not to lose the glass in my hand. A light flickers off a boat in the distance. More vessels will follow when the sun rises over the water.

I'm getting sleepy, but I'm not ready to give up the search just yet. There's just something so addicting to the quest for sea glass. Every find adds to the possibilities of an even greater treasure.

Thirty minutes later, my light hits a piece of glass half hidden in sand. When I bend to retrieve it, my heart skips a beat. A beautiful teal piece meets my gaze. When I turn the glass over in my hand, I notice what looks like a raised number or letter. On closer inspection, I make out the letter "a." I can't believe it. I'm staring at my first initial.

I break out in a happy dance on the beach, hooting and hollering like a crazy person, but I'm alone, so who cares?

I just found my new favorite piece of sea glass.

CJ

Every noise wakes me, so I watch Avery slip out of the loft sometime around midnight. The window faces the water, so I'm not surprised to see her head for the beach. The girl is obsessed with sea glass.

I can't blame her. The frosted glass is beautiful, especially when it catches the light. Her treasures line the windowsill. If I could find enough pieces, I'd make a glass mosaic, but I don't have the needed patience for the search. I'll stick with Amiya and make shell jewelry.

My stomach grumbles. A late-night snack is calling my name. The kitchen is dark, so I pad across the floorboards to the refrigerator. Cold air greets me when I open the door, trying to decide if I want leftover chicken or some grapes.

"Personally, I'm craving chocolate chip cookies." The voice makes me jump. Avery's grandmother is sitting in the recliner in the corner of the living room.

"I didn't see you." I whirl around. If I had food in my hand, it would've flown across the room.

"Sorry to scare you." She stands and turns on the light, making me blink. Apparently, the woman is not worried about waking the others.

"Grab a big bowl." Grams nods to the cabinet under the island.

When she gathers the ingredients, I realize she's not using premade dough. Grams is baking chocolate chip cookies from scratch.

I ask her about her recipe, and she touches her chest. "I know it by heart."

I'm impressed. "I've never made homemade cookies."

"Really?" She looks up from cracking an egg. "My mom refused to make anything from a box. She would turn over in her grave if she knew you could buy cookie dough."

The whole process fascinates me. I've always signed up for art classes, but maybe I should take living skills for my elective classes next year. I overheard some kids talking about how they got to make smoothies and banana pancakes. My mouth waters just thinking about it.

"See if there's a small ice cream scoop with the mixing spoons." Grams points to a container of kitchen utensils near the stove.

I'm confused. I thought we were making cookies, not dishing up ice cream, but I hand her the only scoop I can find—large.

She laughs as she pulls out two cookie sheets. "I guess we're making monster cookies."

When Grams digs into the dough, I realize the scoop is to make the cookies uniform in size. "Brilliant," I mutter.

Nine perfect balls fit on each cookie sheet.

"The secret is to take the cookies out early and let them finish baking on the pan." Grams slips her hand into a potholder. "Most people overbake cookies."

Ten minutes later, the delicious smell permeates the whole house. The screen door opens as I pull out the first pan from the oven.

Avery takes in the scene. The flour dusting my apron, the mixer on the counter, the empty package of chocolate chips.

"Want some cookie dough?" Grams hands Avery one of the beaters. "We put in extra chocolate chips."

Hurt flickers in her eyes.

I feel guilty. Like I've just been caught.

We . . . me and Grams. Not Avery and Grams.

This is not my grandmother.

Shame follows the guilt.

Once again, I'm the imposter in the family.

Avery

Grams loves everyone. Of course, she would welcome CJ as one of her own grandchildren. Her heart's that big.

I just didn't expect to find the two of them bonding in the kitchen. The sting still hurts even though the cookie dough helped.

"What'd you find?" Grams wipes her hands on her apron.

"It's an A." I hold up the teal piece to the light.

"Ooh," she squeals. "A mystery. I wonder what was written on the bottle?"

I've been pondering the question since I found the sea glass. "The 'a' is lowercase, so I'm guessing it wasn't the first letter, but the word could be anything."

"Quite fitting with your first name."

I trace a finger over the raised glass.

"What about you, CJ? What do your initials stand for?"

"Promise you won't laugh?"

Grams crosses her chest.

"Clementine Juliette."

The name sounds old—not something I expected. "Is it a family name?"

CJ shakes her head. "It's the name of a character."

"I love it." Grams claps. "What book?"

"Clementine Juliette was my mom's imaginary friend when she was a girl and the star of my bedtime stories. My mom scribbled her ideas on napkins and sticky notes, hoping to get published someday. She wanted my dad to illustrate the stories."

"Fascinating." Grams smiles. "I can't wait to read about her adventures."

"Me, too." Sadness fills CJ's voice.

She doesn't talk about her past.

What is she not saying?

CJ

After our chocolate chip binge fest, I sleep through breakfast. I wander outside, a mug of coffee in one hand and my sketchbook in the other.

My fingers are already itching. The bay is full of sailboats. I can't wait to capture this on paper. I settle on the Adirondack chair that's become my spot. My mom found a pair at a garage sale when I was younger. I can still see my dad painting the two chairs a beautiful aqua color while my mom sat cross-legged on the deck sipping lemonade and watching him. The two were inseparable.

Mike asks if I want to kayak. He heads to the shed when he can't convince me. I didn't kayak at camp; I'm not kayaking now.

From the safety of the deck, I watch Mike and Avery carry the kayaks to the water's edge. The bright colors against the blue water strike my creativity.

"You really should try." Grams joins me. "There's just something about being so close to the water, like you're at one with nature."

I am a little curious.

"You don't have to go out far." She adjusts her straw hat. "Trust me. You won't regret it."

Ten minutes later, I have my serious doubts.

Amiya is practically doing cartwheels; she's so excited to join her dad in a tandem kayak. But I'm shaking like I have withdrawals.

Why did I let myself get suckered into this?

"Take a few deep breaths." Grams tightens my life jacket. "You'll have fun."

My heart pounds in my chest. This is a bad idea. I'm not a strong swimmer. *What if we tip? What if the thing takes on water?*

"You can go with Avery." Mike points to another tandem. "She's been kayaking since she could swim."

Really? He wants me to trust his daughter. The girl hates me. *What if she tries to drown me?*

"We'll all be together." Mike adjusts his ball cap. "You'll do great."

Again, I'm not convinced.

I'm officially insane. A sensible person would listen to the voice screaming in her head. *Run while you can.*

But if there's one thing I've learned in foster care. Don't show them your weakness. So even though every fiber inside me protests, I force myself to be strong.

My life jacket pinches which is good. I want the thing as tight as possible. I can swim in a pool where I can see the bottom. This is the ocean. Or close enough. Puget Sound stretches for miles in every direction.

Mike pointed out the Space Needle when we got here yesterday. When I looked through his binoculars to the opposite shore, I couldn't believe I was staring at the famous Seattle landmark.

At least there's no wind, so the water appears calm. But looks can be deceiving.

Mike and Avery position the kayak. The thing looks like a child's flimsy plastic toy—not a substantial watercraft able to withstand waves.

"Climb in," Mike urges me when I hesitate.

A wave of cold water engulfs my feet when I step forward, making me shiver. A small fish hits my ankle, making me jump.

Mike laughs. "That little thing won't hurt you."

Maybe not but I can't let my mind think about what else lurks under the surface, or I'll never do this thing.

"Stay low," Mike coaches me as I grip the sides and step into the kayak, my knuckles stark white against the bright red plastic.

Maybe I'd be more comfortable in a canoe. The kayak sits so low in the water, I feel like a duck riding the waves when I take my seat and tuck my legs under the front.

"Here you go." Mike hands me an oar and gives me the basics on how to paddle. I try to concentrate, but Avery steps inside, and the kayak sways.

Good thing I didn't eat breakfast. Otherwise, the fish would be feasting on the chunks spewing from my mouth.

Avery takes her place, and the kayak lurches as Mike pushes us off. I force myself not to bail while the water is still shallow.

"Looking good," Olivia cheers from the shore. She and Grams look smaller by the second as Avery paddles further out.

"You okay?" Mike glides beside us. Amiya is grinning from ear to ear in the front seat.

I manage a squeaky yes. I haven't even attempted to paddle. Avery's doing all the work.

Good thing, breathing doesn't require thought. If it weren't for my automatic nervous system controlling this important matter, I would forget.

"You can let go of the sides." Mike points to the oar resting across my legs. "Match what Avery does."

I stick my oar in the water, but I hurt our efforts more than help.

Mike gives me some pointers and praises me when I catch on. I can't help but smile. My heart rate finally slows to enjoy the experience. Maybe I can do this thing after all.

Amiya is bored, so Mike salutes me before paddling toward shore. "Good job, CJ. You look like a pro."

Avery takes in the surroundings. Her face is relaxed under her bucket hat.

"I love the sound of the water lapping against the side of the kayak. This is my happy place."

I don't know if I'd go that far. But I can appreciate the incredible view. Nature is pure art.

"You're doing good."

The compliment is unexpected.

"I never thanked you." Avery turns to look me in the eye. "You saved my sister."

I'm not good when it comes to admitting my mistakes, but I owe her an apology. "I'm sorry about the picture I posted."

"You're not the only one who needs to apologize," Avery admits. "I found my bobble head. I shouldn't have accused you."

I don't know what to do, so I give her a fist bump.

Avery cocks an eyebrow. "Don't you just love awkward moments?"

We both laugh, releasing the tension.

"I'm sorry for being a jerk," Avery says. "I haven't exactly been easy to live with."

"True that!"

"Hey!" She threatens to splash me with water. "You didn't have to agree so fast."

"Truce," I hurry to say. "My attitude hasn't been much better. Foster care has made me a little jaded."

"Look!" Avery exclaims. "It's a pair of seals."

Their spotted heads bob in the water. I can't believe we're so close.

"They're playing." Avery pulls her phone from the waterproof lanyard around her neck and snaps a picture. "Isn't that sweet?"

I can't help but laugh at their funny whiskers. "The seals were my dad's favorite at the zoo."

"I love the monkeys."

"Me, too," I admit, and we both exchange a look.

"We actually have something in common?" Avery exaggerates her speech.

I would splash her, but I'm lost in memory. Visiting the huge aquarium at the zoo, my brother atop my dad's shoulders as stingrays and sharks glide past us. I can still hear my brother laugh at the funny antics of the penguins and the feel of the giraffe's tongue against my hand when I fed him pellets. We ended with ice cream drizzled in chocolate sauce and sprinkles—Toby's favorite. If there was a perfect day, this is mine.

"We should probably head back," Avery breaks my thoughts. I blink, realizing the seals have disappeared under water.

I take the oar again, feeling more confident. It's not too hard once you get the hang of the rhythm.

I let myself relax enough to watch a seagull dive for fish. When he comes up with a nice silver specimen which glints in the sun, I'm amazed at the bird's agility and skill.

"That's what you call fresh sushi." Avery laughs.

I resist the urge to kiss the ground when we hit the shore. I'm alive, even though my legs feel like spaghetti.

Mike slaps me on the back of my life jacket. "How was it?"

Avery watches my reaction.

"I'd go kayaking again," I find myself admitting. "It was fun."

A smile spreads across Avery's face, but she says nothing of our truce.

And then I'm talking about the seals and the seagull and the fish, and I realize I haven't talked this much since I moved into my new foster home.

Any foster home, actually.

Mike raises his eyebrows. "Sounds like the girl is hooked."

"Maybe." I grab the end of the kayak to carry it back to the shed with Avery.

"I'm proud of you, kid."

The look in Mike's eye reminds me of my dad. Something tells me he'd be beaming, too.

Avery

CJ and I stay up late talking, keeping our voices low so as not to wake Amiya. I think of sleepovers with Lucia where we stay up all night.

Turns out we have more in common than I realized. We both love Thai food, Hot Cheetos, dark chocolate, mango smoothies, Mountain Dew and boba tea. We don't like algebra or cats, and we both want a Jeep when we learn to drive.

"You're always sketching." I turn on my stomach and hug my pillow under my chin. "What do you draw?"

"Anything." She shrugs. "It helps me relax."

"Can I see your artwork?"

CJ hesitates, no doubt wondering if I can be trusted.

"Please."

Something in my voice must be convincing because CJ nudges the sketchbook toward me. "This is one from our trip."

I sit up on the bed and study her sketch. The shading makes the driftwood look so realistic; I want to trace the knots on the wood with my fingertip. I'm staring at a work of art.

"Wow," I mutter. "This is amazing."

"It's my first attempt at a landscape."

"Really? Where did you learn to draw?"

"My dad was an artist." Her voice gets quieter. "I wanted to be just like him."

I want to ask questions, but I'm afraid of the answers. CJ is in foster care for a reason.

"He died in a car accident."

"Oh, wow." I gulp. "I had no idea."

She purses her lips together. "I don't talk about it much."

Silence hangs in the air while I flip through her other sketches. I think of my own pathetic stick figures and am blown away by CJ's talent. "These are incredible."

She criticizes herself for things I don't see.

"You're too hard on yourself."

Midway through the sketch book, I stop at a picture of a toddler like the one I found in the treehouse. He looks just like CJ.

"Is that your . . ."

"Little brother," she finishes.

More questions fill my mind. How old is he? Is her brother in foster care, too? Does CJ get to see him on visits with her mom?

"He died in the car accident with my father."

Her words cut like a knife. I'm completely at a loss for what to say.

"I . . . I'm so sorry."

CJ exhales. "It was three years ago, but it feels like yesterday. The pain never really goes away."

I keep thinking of Amiya and the choking incident. Little siblings are annoying, but they're also wonderful. I can't imagine life without Amiya.

"His name was Toby," CJ finally says. "And he was obsessed with dinosaurs and fire trucks."

She smiles as she tells me about how he insisted their mom make an extra peanut butter and jelly sandwich (cut into triangles) at lunch for his favorite toy, a large plastic T-Rex figure named Sammy.

"Aren't they carnivores?"

"Apparently not the plastic species." CJ laughs. "French fries were also a favorite and equally entertaining. Every trip to McDonalds meant we bought extra fries for Sammy."

I picture a plastic dinosaur on the table at a booth in the restaurant and imagine a little guy putting a fry between the dinosaur's teeth.

"My dad would distract Toby and then eat the fry." CJ smiles. "And my brother fell for it every time. He was convinced the T-Rex loved French fries."

CJ pulls a photograph from her pocket. "Here's my family."

I don't know what I'm expecting, but her family looks so normal. Their love for each other is obvious.

Maybe it's the ball cap or the boyish looks, but her father looks like a cross between an athlete and a country singer. His lean frame is draped across CJ's mother—a pretty thing with a natural, earthy beauty. A straw hat tops long chestnut hair. CJ is sandwiched between her dad and her little brother, a cute kid in a dinosaur tank top. A Shih Tzu tries to lick the red lollipop in his hand.

I always figured her parents were awful people. Why else would CJ be in foster care?

"I don't blame my mother," CJ reads my mind. "The accident broke her heart. She hasn't been the same since."

No wonder CJ has anger issues. Her entire world shattered. No foster family could ever replace her parents or her little brother.

"Your dog's cute. What's his name?"

"Oscar." She smiles, taking back the photograph. "He was always at Toby's side, ready to eat anything he dropped. See how he was sharing my little brother's lollipop."

I laugh. I want to ask where the dog is, but I don't want to bring up more pain. For the first time, I see things from CJ's point of view. Foster care means getting ripped away from everything familiar.

For just a moment, our eyes lock. CJ is probably just as surprised.

Something shifts between us.

We slip downstairs to get a snack and find Grams in the kitchen. Am I imagining things, or do her pajamas seem like they hang off her?

"I thought I heard your whispers drifting down from the loft. Would you like a steamer?"

CJ takes a bar stool. "What's a steamer?"

"Sweetened warm milk with a frothy top."

"Did we wake you?" I take a seat beside CJ as Grams pulls the caramel syrup from the pantry.

"No, I haven't been sleeping well."

Before I can ask questions, Grams explains how to make a steamer. CJ is hooked from her first sip. "How have I missed this experience?"

"Good, huh?"

CJ licks the froth from her lips. "Amazing."

We move to the couches, and the next half hour disappears as we talk about the day and CJ's first experience kayaking.

"Look at the water droplets beading their whiskers." I pull up the pictures of the seals. "They almost look like they're posing."

I scroll through other pictures on my phone—me and Lucia on the last day of school, my award ceremony for track, and a pool party with my friends.

Like always, Grams wants every detail. At some point, CJ falls asleep, so Grams covers her with a blanket.

I should do the same, so I hug her good night. She's so thin, brittle. "Is everything okay?"

Grams shakes her head, her eyes filling with tears. "There's no easy way to say this."

The ominous words make my blood chill.

"I . . . I have breast cancer."

Her words hit hard.

A sucker punch that sends my world spinning. Just when I was warming to the foster girl, my life shifts underneath me.

Again.

I thrive on order and predictability.

The unknown terrifies me.

"It's not bad, right?" I choke out. "You can beat this thing."

She manages to smile. "That's my plan. I'm not going out without a fight."

My knees buckle, and I fall to the couch. CJ jolts up when I hit her leg.

Her eyes dart wildly about. "What happened?"

"We're so sorry." Grams brushes back a strand of hair, making me wonder how long until she loses her long grey-white locks. "We didn't mean to wake you."

I must look awful because CJ's face softens. "What's wrong?"

"I have cancer, sweetie," Grams says quietly. "I just told Avery the news."

Something like the sound of a wounded animal escapes her lips, but she says nothing.

"I don't want to ruin our vacation, but I wanted to tell you in person." She squeezes my hand. "I need my number one cheerleader rooting for me."

Leave it to my grandmother to look on the bright side. Grams can't shed her positive outlook, even if she's dying.

"It's going to be a battle, but the doctor says I have a real good chance."

"I'll change my flight home. I'm sure Mom and Dad will let me stay for the summer."

"Aren't you babysitting?"

"I'll talk to Lucia. She's looking for a job."

CJ is quiet.

"Every day is a gift." Grams takes me in her arms. "I want to focus on living."

I feel like a big baby, but I can't help crying.

I can't imagine my world without Grams.

CJ

I want to say something, but there are no words.
Empty words are the worst anyway.
Humans have a hard time with silence.
Quiet terrifies us.

It's worse when something bad happens. We have no idea what to say, so we try to fill the emptiness with stupid clichés or meaningless words to avoid the silence and the awkwardness.

That's what happened when my dad died.

The only people who really got it were those who had suffered their own loss. They didn't try to fix anything. They listened if I wanted to talk. Or said nothing if I was silent.

They were just there.
Present.

I vow to do the same for Grams and Avery. Cancer doesn't equal a death sentence, but I'm sure the diagnosis still feels the same because of all the unknowns.

I squeeze Grams' hand, then Avery's hand. Both respond with a slight pressure to mine as we sit on the couch. Not saying a thing.

Letting the silence stretch out.
And being okay with the quiet.
They'll talk when they're ready.

Avery

I'm guessing this is what a hangover feels like when I wake up to the smell of coffee brewing in the kitchen. My head is pounding, and my stomach is a queasy mess of nerves. I must've fallen asleep on the couch.

For just a moment, I think this is all a bad nightmare, but then I remember the awful words. And I feel like I could throw up.

My dad is scrambling eggs, but I can't stomach food. Emptiness balloons inside me.

I feel so lost.

I'm sitting on the couch in a semi-catatonic stage when Grams approaches. I look like I haven't slept. She looks refreshed in a sundress that falls to her ankles.

"Come on, get dressed." She nudges my shoulder to rouse me. "We're going thrifting."

My grandmother is the queen of thrifting. We could spend hours rummaging through bins and sifting through shelves of trinkets looking for that perfect find. My all-time favorite treasure is a four-foot-tall wooden giraffe which stands at my bedroom door greeting me. Black tribal prints run the length of its long neck.

I try to protest, but Grams is insistent.

"Shouldn't we talk to my parents about me staying for the summer?"

"Later." Grams grabs her keys. "I'll be waiting in the car."

Five minutes later, I open the door on my grandparents' Highlander and slide into the front passenger seat.

"No cancer talk today." Grams turns up the radio—an oldies rock station—and sings along with *Faithfully* by Journey as she pulls out of the Airbnb.

The music works its magic, and by the time, we pull up to the thrift store, I'm ready to shop.

"Let's do this." Grams grabs her purse, her eyes sparkling. No one would suspect cancer. Life oozes from her.

I shouldn't be surprised by my grandmother's enthusiasm. She never acts her age. Why would she act like she's dying?

Grams opens the car door. "I'm thinking lunch after we shop. What do you think?"

My stomach rumbles in answer—a good thing. I actually feel like eating.

Most days, the goal is the hunt. I don't even know what I'm looking for until I see it. But my growing sea glass collection needs a few new containers, so I head for the shelves of odds and ends while Grams checks out the clothes.

I tackle the mission like a James Bond wannabee, but Grams is a professional. She could host a bargain hunting television show. I'm always amazed at what she finds and the corresponding price tag—never more than $10.

My eyes scan a row of glass vases when I lock on something half-hidden behind a picture frame and a wicker basket. A small gasp erupts from my lips. That familiar feeling of excitement wells inside me as I pull the container to the front. I've found a gem amongst the sea of discarded odds and ends.

"It's perfect," I mutter, as I turn the unique glass container over in my hands. It's shaped like a fish with raised glass fins and a cork plugged in the mouth. The glass is cool against my flesh. I can already imagine filling it with different colored sea glass.

Grams finds me in the aisle. A pair of pants and a shirt are draped across her arm. "Sorry, I got distracted in the clothing section."

I smile. My grandmother could be a model, and she never spends more than a few dollars on an outfit—even though she looks like a million bucks.

"Look what I found." I lift the fish container, and the light glints off the glass.

"What a find." She whistles. "Add some fish net and a few shells, and you could make a neat display."

The idea pulls at my imagination.

"Look at that." Grams points to a blue bottle with a long neck.

I cradle the bottle. My bigger pieces won't fit through the neck, but it's perfect for all the smaller pieces. The blue will add a nice tint to all my clear pieces.

I could spend another hour browsing the shelves, but I can see Grams is tired, even if she's trying to hide her exhaustion.

"Ready for lunch?"

Grams looks grateful as we head for the register. "Shopping always gives me an appetite."

Ten minutes later, we opt for outdoor seating at a local seafood place on the water. Grams orders a tuna salad, and I opt for the fish and chips.

"I'm so glad you're here." She takes a sip of iced tea. "I've been counting the days down for weeks."

I can't help but wonder if the doctor has given her a countdown, but I promised not to talk about the cancer.

"What?" Grams takes a deep breath, enjoying the slight breeze under the umbrella. "I can see your mind spinning."

"It's nothing."

"You're not a good liar. And I know it's killing you not to ask about the cancer." Grams laughs at the expression on my face at her poor choice of words.

"I'm sorry. Forgive me for my gallows humor."

If only I could have the same attitude.

"What are the odds?" I sit on my hands to keep them from shaking. "I mean, did the doctor say anything?"

"I'm not a spring chicken." Grams leans forward, holding my hands. "Something else could kill me, so I'm not going to focus on the odds. God ordained the number of my days."

I swallow, trying to keep back the emotion as the server brings our food.

"So . . ." Grams pauses, hazel eyes meeting mine. "This idea of you staying with me over the summer. Does it have anything to do with avoiding CJ?"

"No." My voice squeaks, giving me away.

My grandmother crosses her arms, waiting for me to be honest. She expects nothing less—even when the truth is hard to face.

"Maybe a little," I admit. "But me and CJ agreed to a truce out kayaking. I really want to be with you."

"Papa and I could use the help." She rests a hand on mine. "Let's talk to your parents."

She gets excited, thinking about trips to the beach and the thrifting we'll do, but I don't voice my doubts.

I'm staying the summer to help her fight cancer.

I need to be strong.

Brace myself for the rough days ahead.

CJ

It's silly—even childish—but I keep hoping I'll find a message in a bottle on the beach since this is my first visit to the ocean. When the others look for shells or sea glass, I scan the sand, looking under driftwood for a bottle with a cork.

My dad was the artist, but my mom was the storyteller. Her elaborate stories fueled my imagination with fantastic creatures and characters on quests for treasure or lost cities.

One of my favorite Clementine Juliette stories centered around her discovery of a coded message in a bottle on a riverbank. She unlocked the code to discover a cave filled with ancient hieroglyphs.

I don't have any luck finding a message in a bottle, so I sit on a piece of driftwood with my sketchbook. At first, I don't know what I'm drawing, but my subconscious takes over and a picture emerges. I shouldn't be surprised when Dad and Toby stare back at me.

Maybe I could put this sketch in a bottle. My dad and brother would love the idea.

I'm not sure what to write, so I settle on a quote from my favorite childhood book: *Guess How Much I Love You*.

> D & T: I love you both to the moon and back. And I miss you that much, too. CJ

Now I just need a bottle. I add the date and my email just in case someone finds my sketch.

I pull up Google on my phone, curious about the best way to launch a bottle so it doesn't return with the waves. Of course, I get lost in the stories I discover.

I'm intrigued by the following message found by a Dutch couple in Oosterschelde, Netherlands, in 2013.

Dear finder, my name is Zoe Lemon. Please would you write to me, I would like it a lot. I am 10 years old and I like ballet, playing the flute and the piano. I have a hamster called Sparkle and fish called Speckle.

Zoe was traveling by ferry on holiday from England to Belgium when she threw a plastic bottle overboard. Twenty-three years later at Christmas, her parents received a letter from the couple who found the bottle while looking for interesting debris.

A ferry. I never thought about that as an option instead of launching the bottle from the shore. We're taking the ferry to San Juan Island tomorrow.

Goosebumps rise to my flesh as my imagination takes over.

There are more stories.

A message written by a 5-year-old.

A note from a former soldier in the Vietnamese Army who attempted to escape the communist regime.

A letter penned by a 26-year-old World War I soldier to his wife on his way to fight in France in September of 1914. Two days after writing the note,

Private Thomas Hughes was killed in battle. The letter was delivered 85 years later to his daughter.

A message in a bottle from a 21-year-old American soldier in 1945 that was found by an 18-year-old milk maid in Ireland. They exchanged letters for 7 years before finally meeting.

A note written by a French mother broken over the death of her 13-year-old son Maurice brings tears to my eyes.

While on a ferry crossing the English Channel in 2002, she threw some clothes and lilies overboard, along with a teardrop-shaped bottle with the following message.

Forgive me for being so angry at your disappearance. I still think there's been some mistake, and I keep waiting for God to fix it . . . Forgive me for not having known how to protect you from death. Forgive me for not having been able to find the words at that terrible moment when you slipped through my fingers.

That one gets to me.

I'm the big sister.

My little brother's protector, and I let him slip through my fingers.

Avery

I thought I would need pie charts and graphs to convince my parents of the merits of me staying with Grams over the summer, but they immediately agreed.

If Mom could get off work, she would stay longer, but our vacation took most of her paid time off. So, me staying behind while Grams begins her treatment eases their worry.

Papa tries to help, but his back injury has made physical activity difficult. And Grams has always been the cook. They'd live on scrambled eggs and mac 'n cheese if he took over the kitchen. And Grams can't beat this thing if she doesn't eat her veggies and whole grains.

Amiya needs more convincing.

"I want to help Grams, too."

I don't want to burst her bubble, but my little sister still believes in monsters under her bed. If she stayed, I would be caring for her and Grams both.

"It's not fair," Amiya pouts, her lower lip jutting out in defiance. "I'm going to be a first grader."

I kneel before her and tuck a stray lock of hair behind her ears. "Who will take care of Lola if we're both gone?"

My question makes Amiya pause. Her lips twist as she considers Lola's plight.

I push my own feelings aside. Not being with my furry friend will be the hardest part of staying back, but Grams is my priority.

Amiya lights up. "Can Lola sleep with me?"

Our dog usually curls up in my full-sized bed, so she may protest a change. "You might need to sleep in my bed. Lola will need you."

That convinces Amiya. She's needed at home while I'm in Washington.

"I promise to take good care of Lola." She squeezes me in a big hug. "Cross my heart."

Poor Lola will be subjected to tea parties and dress up sessions every day, but my sister is happy. Amiya trots off to tell my parents the plan.

Crisis averted.

CJ

A plastic bottle just isn't the same as glass, so I ask if we can make a quick pit stop at the thrift store before we head to the ferry.

When I emerge with an old clear bottle topped with a cork, Mike assumes I want to add shells or sea glass.

I don't correct him.

Some things aren't meant to be shared.

I couldn't find any jute twine, but a rubber band should work well. We're 15 miles out from the ferry, but Amiya is doing the potty dance. When we stop, I uncork the bottle while everyone is occupied. The rolled-up sketch fits perfectly.

I hug the glass bottle close.

Everything was such a blur after the accident. The funeral. The burial. The shock.

Something my therapist said comes to mind.

"Grief isn't something you get over. Grief is something you learn to live with."

It's time to finally say goodbye.

Avery

"Remember our last trip to San Juan Island?" Grams asks me when we board the ferry.

How could I forget. Papa and Grams took us on a whale watching excursion that still ranks in my top memories of all time.

We talk about how close our boat got to the orcas, and how fascinated we were every time they breached the water. One of the pictures I took is the screensaver on my laptop. The stark black and white coloring of the orcas stands out against the blue water.

The guide told us about two ecotypes commonly found in the Salish Sea—the transient orcas and the critically endangered Southern Residents named the J, K and L pods. I was amazed at how the guide could even identify several individual whales by their saddle patches, scars on their dorsal fins or nicks on their flukes.

"Remember the dog who could smell whale poop?" I laugh, thinking about the small research craft which moored near us in the water. The scientists studying the orcas used the pooch to help locate the orcas in the water.

My excitement grows at the sound of the ferry wheel churning as we leave the dock at Anacortes. Even though we're not whale watching today when we land at Friday Harbor, exploring San Juan Island is always fun. There's a bakery we always visit along with a great seafood place.

I stand on the deck, watching for signs of harbor seals and sea lions. A bald eagle flies overhead. The water laps against the side of the ferry, the misty spray touching my face.

"Our last trip here, we missed the ferry, so Papa surprised me with a 10-minute seaplane ride into the island." Grams lights up. "What a treat! The view from above was incredible."

I want to ask more, but a pair of porpoises entertains us. My phone almost goes overboard in my excitement. Amiya thinks they're orcas, but someone in the crowd says they're Dall's porpoises.

A quick Google search reveals that the chunky porpoises often get mistaken for orcas because of their black and white coloring. Unlike orcas, however, Dall's porpoises don't have eye or saddle patches and their small dorsal fins are more triangular versus the hooked fin of the orca, which can get up to six feet tall in males. I still remember my surprise when I found out orcas weren't whales, but dolphins.

The hour-long ride feels like minutes when we pull up to the pier. My legs feel a little wobbly stepping onto land, but I'm ready to explore.

CJ

I've never been on a boat before, so I feel like a little kid. Toby would love the ferry. I can just imagine him having a blast.

Amiya begs her mother to go to the top, but she sits on a bench, very pale. Apparently, Olivia forgot her Dramamine. The poor thing looks ready to hurl.

"I'll take her." I follow Amiya up the stairs to the top deck where the view takes my breath away. I need my sketchbook.

"I hope we see a sea lion." Amiya climbs on the rail, her hair whipping in the wind.

"But you don't want to swim with them." I pull her off the rail before she falls. Toby would do the same. The kid was fearless.

Seagulls fly overhead while water laps against the hull, mesmerizing me. I subconsciously touch the straps on my backpack, wondering if my bottle will find its way to shore.

The statistics for someone to discover a message in a bottle must be like winning the lottery, but I'm just crazy enough to believe in this little experiment.

Will someone respond? Will the hope keep the memory of my dad and Toby alive?

Amiya wants to explore, so I consider my options as we walk around the length of the ferry. I wonder about the wind. The last thing I want is my bottle to get caught in a gust and shatter against the side.

That makes me feel guilty about littering until I think of Avery's sea glass and remember how the ocean makes art from broken glass. Maybe I'm just justifying my crime, but it's enough to ease my conscience.

Avery walks toward us, so I pass off Amiya, making up an excuse to go the bathroom and slip around the other side of the ferry. Judging by our expected arrival, I figure we're at the halfway point in our crossing—the farthest point from either shore.

Now would be the ideal time to launch. As I pull the bottle from my bag, a memory comes to mind.

Toby inherited a plastic tub full of Hot Wheels and racetracks from Dad who collected the little metal cars as a kid. The launcher fascinated my brother, so the two made a game of launching the cars into a box. Every time one of the Hot Wheels landed in the box, Toby would pump his little fist and yell, "Yes!" The game entertained them for hours.

A seagull lands on the rail, bringing me back to the present. Tears wet my lashes as I grasp the bottle. The last three years have been the hardest days of my life, but I can't hold onto the anger forever. Dad and Toby would want me to move on.

"I miss you both so much." I heave the glass with all my strength. The waves are too loud to hear a splash and the distance too great to see, but I imagine the bottle hitting the water where the light glints off the surface.

I stare at the spot in the ferry's wake, not moving until San Juan Island comes into view.

When I step back onto land, I feel lighter.

At peace.

Avery

CJ's been quiet since our return from San Juan Island. I know I'm always in a funk when vacation comes to an end.

Papa puts my suitcase in the Highlander while Dad loads the rental car. We'll follow them to the airport to say our goodbyes because Grams wants to spend the day in Seattle before returning to their home in Bremerton.

I forget my phone charger in the loft, so I head inside. CJ is sitting on the bed, her suitcase packed beside her.

"Uh, are you okay?" I say awkwardly, feeling like I've invaded her privacy.

"Fine." She jerks her head to the wall, but not before I see the tears.

I grab my charger and disappear down the stairs.

Just when I feel like we could be close, CJ pushes me away. She lost her brother and her father. What if Grams doesn't make it? I could use someone who understands.

The irony feels like a slap in the face.

I would've given anything to move in with my grandparents a month ago. I wanted nothing more than to escape CJ.

But not under these circumstances.

Not watching my grandmother suffer.

It's probably best that me and CJ will be living a part for the summer.

Maybe this whole foster sister thing was never meant to work.

CJ

Foster care comes with little privacy. Even if you're lucky enough to have your own room, you get put together with strangers who are supposed to be your family.

But they aren't.

Not really.

Like with me and Avery. She's my latest foster sister after the twins. Before them, there was the K crew—five sisters all with K names.

So just because me and Avery had a few bonding moments doesn't mean anything.

Not really.

Or at least that's what I tell myself because now she's staying with her grandparents for the rest of the summer and we're saying goodbye.

I didn't want Avery to see the tears.

I'm not ready to leave Puget Sound or Grams and Papa . . . or Avery. I was just starting to believe things would be different.

Serves me right for opening my heart just to have it crushed again.

I don't want Grams to go through cancer treatments, but a little part of me is jealous of the close bond Avery has with her grandmother.

I never had that with my own grandparents. My mom's mother has dementia. Her father and my dad's parents have been deceased for years.

Me staying behind in Washington won't work anyway. Not if I want to have visits with my mom.

And I can't lose her.

Even if it feels like she's already lost.

All this is going through my head on our drive to the airport in Seattle. I try to sleep, but my mind won't shut off.

We return the rental and meet Avery, Grams and Papa at the terminal where we say our goodbyes. Amiya doesn't want to let go of Avery, so I pull her gently away and wrap my arms around her. She buries her face in my waist and cries.

"Thanks," Avery mouths. "Take care of her."

I nod. It's so weird that I'm going to be the substitute big sis to Amiya for the summer.

Grams hasn't shed a single tear. I'm guessing she's trying to be brave for everyone. No one asks the question, but it's hard not to wonder if this is the last goodbye.

I don't know which is harder: dreading the inevitable or being surprised by the sudden.

I barely remember my last moments with my dad or Toby. Everyone else was finishing lunch when I stumbled into the kitchen.

"Nice of you to wake up." My dad kissed me on the head as I grabbed the box of Lucky Charms.

"It's Saturday," I mumbled, not giving them hugs before Dad strapped Toby in the car seat to run an errand.

If only I'd said, "I love you."

Not saying goodbye makes closure even harder.

But this is just as difficult.

The time ticking down. Seven of us standing in a crowd, people rushing toward airport security. Knowing we need to leave so we don't miss our plane. Wanting to say something profound yet not knowing what to say.

And lingering in the moment—trying somehow to beat time.

Avery

I figure Grams wants to get fresh flowers and homegrown vegetables at Pike Place, but she surprises me with her announcement.

"I got us tickets to Seattle's Underground Tour." She buckles into the driver's seat and sets the GPS to Pioneer Square.

"We've talked about going for years, but haven't taken the time," Grams explains as she pulls into traffic. "So why not?"

Papa turns in the front passenger seat to explain. "The underground tour is a historic walk underneath Seattle's oldest neighborhood."

"It's probably not what you think about as bucket list material." Grams laughs. "But this whole cancer diagnosis is making me look at time differently. I'm not going to put off anything any longer."

I shift in my seat. I don't like talking about bucket lists and cancer, but I can't ignore the subject either—not if I'm here to support my grandmother through this journey.

"A friend of mine had a blast on the tour, so I promised myself to go at the next chance."

An hour later, we're listening to our tour guide talk about how the abandoned spaces under the city's shops and restaurants were built after the Great Seattle Fire destroyed more than 25 blocks of stores, 4 wharves, and all the city's railroad terminals on June 6, 1889. Surprisingly, only one life was lost, though an estimated one million rats died in the flames, solving Seattle's pest problem.

Of course, Papa gets a kick out of that fact. He raises his hands to his neck, pretending to be a rat choking on smoke.

"Behave," Grams whispers, but he just winks at me. I stifle a laugh so I don't interrupt our guide.

City leaders raised the streets 22 feet higher and required all new structures to be built of stone and brick. Most underground locations began to deteriorate when they were abandoned in 1907 for fear of the bubonic plague. But the passageways came to life again during the Prohibition when people used the secret establishments for gambling, opium dens and speakeasies.

"What's a speakeasy?" I overhear a kid ask his dad.

"An illegal liquor store or nightclub. Alcohol sales were prohibited in 1920s."

A teenage boy says something under his breath which makes his friends laugh.

We head below street level to a series of interconnected passageways. Good thing I changed my flip flops for tennis shoes because the terrain is a bit rugged. The lighting is dim, though skylights above definitely help. I find myself getting lost in history, like I'm transported back in time. The whole thing is unusual, but interesting.

A little over an hour later, I blink when we emerge from underground. Grams is tired and pale, but happy. She thanks me for being a good sport. Papa is in worse shape with his back, so we find a restaurant for lunch.

"We're quite the pair." Grams slips into a booth and downs an entire glass of water. "You sure you want to hang out with two old people for the summer?"

I can't think of anything I'd rather do.

Papa lifts his glass and clinks mine. "To summer."

Grams lifts her empty glass. She grins, but I can see the worry in her eyes.

I hope the waver in my voice isn't noticeable. I can't focus on my own anxiety. My grandparents need me to be strong.

"To summer."

CJ

A storm wakes me up, so I pad over to the window in my bare feet and stare outside. I've always been fascinated by the way raindrops bead on glass before trailing down the windowpane.

Amiya barges into my room holding her blanket. Lola follows close at her heels. "I'm scared."

I reach out my arms, and she snuggles close. Of course, Lola wants in the action, so the little terrier wiggles into the small space.

"Did the thunder wake you up?"

She nods. The faint scent of her strawberry shampoo fills my nostrils.

"I could tell you a story of the brave princess."

My night light illuminates her bright eyes as we snuggle under the covers. "I love princesses."

"Clementine Juliette is no ordinary princess," I recite the opening lines my mom used to begin every Clementine Juliette adventure. "She is a warrior princess."

Amiya is enraptured as memory transports me back in time.

My mom's touch as she played with my hair.

The whiff of her perfume lingering on her skin.

The sound of her voice rising and falling with the action.

I get lost in the story as I weave together an elaborate tale of Clementine Juliette battling a sea creature who threatens the fishermen and women in a small island village. Our recent vacation helps the details come alive as I describe the sounds of the waves and the smell of the salty air.

Of course, Clementine Juliette overcomes the insurmountable obstacles that threaten to overpower her, and the villagers are grateful for her help.

"But this isn't the last adventure for our fearless warrior princess," I end the story the same way my mom always did. "The brave and beautiful Clementine Juliette will be back for more."

Amiya claps, begging for another story.

"It's late, and the storm's over."

She reluctantly agrees, surprising me with a kiss on the cheek. "Thanks, CJ. I'm glad you're my sister."

Amiya doesn't head back to her own room; she and Lola bury their bodies under my covers. In seconds, both are snoring.

I can't help but smile as I whisper, "Good night."

I don't know if I'm dreaming or half-awake, but sometime in the middle of the night, an idea hits.

I can't wait to tell my mom. Three days until our next visit.

Avery

Grams has been to the doctor multiple times since her diagnosis, but my first trip with her to the doctor is brutal.

I've never been good when it comes to blood. I fainted at the dentist once when I saw the bloody gauze from a loose tooth.

Needles are even worse.

So, when Grams gets her blood drawn, I brace myself. Slow deep breaths.

Inhale.

Exhale.

I need to focus on something other than the needle and the red liquid filling the vial, so I grasp my sea glass bracelet, being mindful of the cool glass against my flesh. The frosted colors. The silver wire encircling each glass charm.

Inhale.

Exhale.

The whole thing is overwhelming.

Learning about the treatment plan. Grams getting weighed and her height measured to determine the exact dosage of chemotherapy. I'm glad I brought a journal to take notes. There's so much information.

Poor Papa. He's a wreck. As soon as he learned Grams needs minor surgery to get a port installed, he had to get fresh air.

I listen to the oncologist explain how the port will eliminate the need for Grams to have an IV put into her arm for every round of chemotherapy.

A port sounds like the best option, but that doesn't ease the nerves doing flip flops in my stomach.

"You doing okay?" Grams touches my arm.

Of course, my grandmother is more concerned about others than herself.

I manage to smile, but she can see through me. "Why don't you go check on Papa?"

She's giving me an out, but when I hesitate, Grams insists. "We're almost done here. You can help me read through all the material again when we're back home."

Papa is sitting outside in a sculpture garden for patients and their families. Rose bushes sweeten the air while water trickles down some rocks into a small pond.

He doesn't see me until I take a seat beside him. Tears trail down his face.

I don't know what to say. We sit in silence for several minutes, each lost in thought. Papa has always been the strong one. A person doesn't spend 20 years in the Navy without being tough, so seeing him like this messes with me.

"I can't lose her."

His booming voice is so soft, I almost don't hear the words.

My fingers are trembling, but I put my hand on his, the contrast of his age spots noticeable against my fair skin. It's the only gesture I can manage because I don't trust myself to speak.

"Thank you for being here." His voice shakes. "It means a lot."

I can only nod, my eyes swimming with tears. I feel so helpless. Awkward. Like I'm in the way.

"I don't want her to see me like this." Papa looks at me with red eyes. "But it's okay if we're a mess together."

I lean into him, and he wraps an arm around me. Feeling the strength of his body makes me feel stronger.

I wonder if Papa feels the same because I can feel him relax. His breathing slows as we sit in the garden listening to the gurgle of the water.

Maybe it's okay not to know what to do or what to say.

Just being present.

So, my grandparents aren't alone.

Maybe that's enough.

CJ

We're at Marley's, the rich smell of coffee swirling around us at the high-top table in the corner. The visitation worker takes a seat at a nearby couch.

Mom cradles a caramel macchiato while I sip a white chocolate hot cocoa. I hide my disappointment when she doesn't remember I went to Puget Sound.

Mom stares blankly ahead. She seems more lost than ever.

Small talk falls short. My enthusiasm to share the vacation pictures on my phone fizzled the moment she forgot.

I eye the time. A minute has passed since the last time I checked.

"So . . . I told one of your Clementine Juliette stories to my foster sister, and she loved it."

As soon as the words leave my lips, I regret opening my mouth.

Mom blinks—the only visible change on her face.

"What if I illustrate?" My voice rises with my desperation. "You know, like Dad was planning to do."

I don't realize I'm holding my breath until my eyes start to swim. Even the visitation worker stops writing notes and watches my mom's reaction.

We don't talk for the remainder of the visit. I finish my drink, trying to disguise the lump in my throat. Every swallow hurts.

She finally speaks when I stand to leave.

"I can't, CJ."

I told myself to prepare for this, but still, the rejection hurts. I stuff my hands into my pockets to hide the tremble.

We leave the coffee shop without another word.

Avery

Grams and I call my family from the beach. They're two hours ahead of us, so they're sitting at the dinner table.

Amiya grabs the phone and makes a pouty face over the video screen. She's not happy they're having fish for supper.

"You'd starve here." I laugh. "We eat salmon or fish two or three times a week."

She pretends to gag.

"We miss you." Mom takes the phone and positions the camera so I can see everyone. "Seeing your empty chair was too much, so Dad moved it to the basement."

CJ waves from the side of the table where I normally sit. It's different to see her there, but surprisingly, I'm okay with the arrangement.

A cancer diagnosis has a way of shrinking problems that once seemed so big. Not to minimize those things. It's just that facing death rearranges your priorities.

Lola barks when she hears my voice, so Dad lifts her to the screen. The furry face staring back at me melts my heart.

"Hey, baby girl," I say, and her ears perk up.

Amiya giggles. "She's trying to lick the phone."

Not being able to pet Lola makes me homesick, but Amiya promises to give her some extra love for me.

We talk for another 15 minutes before hanging up, avoiding mention of the treatments. Mom will call later for those details. She and Dad want to shelter my sister as much as possible.

"Need a hug?" Grams gets up from the bench. "I'm sure you're homesick."

"A little," I admit. "But I'll take a hug."

When Grams wraps me in her arms, I know she's lost even more weight. Pounds she doesn't have to lose.

I force myself to keep positive as we head for the parking lot. "How about some ice cream before we head home?"

Grams loves the idea.

Neither one of us says anything about dessert spoiling our dinner.

She's supposed to limit sugar, but if ice cream helps, then I'll insist Grams order a double scoop.

CJ

I'm in a mood.

I haven't touched my sketchbook for three days.

My heart isn't in it.

Not since my visit with my mother.

Lola crawls onto my lap as if sensing my loss. As I stroke her fur, I find myself talking out loud.

"Dad would want her to keep writing," I tell the little terrier. "But what can I do?"

Lola rests her chin on my arm, making me smile. "You're loving the doggie massage, aren't you?"

She answers by snoring.

I don't know if I should be offended that I put Lola to sleep or concerned that I'm talking to a dog.

I lean back on my pillow and stare at the ceiling.

Maybe if Mom saw an illustration of Clementine Juliette . . . just maybe that would motivate her to dream again.

I grab my sketchbook.

Dad was always doodling pictures of Clementine Juliette on scraps of paper or receipts, so my fingers create what I remember.

Fifteen minutes later, I sit back and study the sketch, realizing that I'm staring at a character that looks like a cross between me and my brother. The freckles are definitely Toby's, but the eyes are mine.

My father always said we were his models, but somehow, I never saw the resemblance before.

Avery

The oncologist tells you to expect them, but nothing really prepares you for the first bad day.

The fourth day after the first chemo treatment, I wake up to Papa calling for help. Grams is in the bathroom hugging the toilet retching out her guts. Every part of me wants to cry out. Seeing her drenched in sweat, so weak and helpless on the floor kills me. But I force myself to be strong.

"Can you bring a glass of water and a fresh nightgown?" Papa is trying not to grimace with his back, but bending over is obviously causing him pain.

I hurry to the kitchen. My hands are shaking as I fill the glass. I also grab a mint. Nothing is worse than the vomit aftermath.

Grams is in bed when I return. Perspiration beads her forehead as I help her put on the fresh nightgown. She's too weak to hold the glass, so I tilt it to her dry lips then unwrap the mint.

"Thank you." Her voice is drained. She insists Papa meet his friends for coffee. A group of retired Navy guys play cards at the American Legion several mornings a week.

"Go," she says when he hesitates. "I want to watch a chick flick with Avery."

Papa kisses her on the forehead, the tenderness sweet to witness.

She pats the bed beside her, but I hang back.

"I won't break." Grams teases, so I crawl beside her and lean my head against hers. "Do you want me to make something to eat?"

She shakes her head. "I can't even stomach the thought of food right now."

"Okay," I agree. "But only if you promise to eat something after the movie."

Grams nods, but I have my doubts. Getting her to eat has been the biggest struggle.

I grab the remote. "What sounds good?"

"What's your favorite?"

That's easy. The 1999 classic, *10 Things I Hate about You*.

Grams holds my hand and I hit play, grateful for the escape. The good cry also helps. We go through half a box of tissue by the time the credits roll.

She eats a few bites of toast before falling asleep. When Papa returns, we sit on the deck. Their house sits atop a small hill, giving them a perfect view of the bay. A butterfly flits between three hanging baskets of fuchsia, my grandmother's favorite flowers.

I lean back on the lounge chair. "Who got bragging rights today?"

"Caffy, the dirty cheat." Papa snorts. "The pollywog doesn't deserve the Shellback pin."

I roll my eyes. Papa and his friends love to talk smack. Their games of rummy are serious battles that can last for hours. Winner gets to wear the coveted Shellback pin until the next winner claims the title.

"Sounds like someone is mad he lost his winning streak."

Papa gives a humph. He and Caffy joined the Navy together out of high school, so I've heard dozens of stories of their mischief over the years.

Like the BT punch.

The two friends would send new recruits to the boiler room to ask for a BT punch a.k.a. a solid punch in the arm from one of the boiler techs.

Papa launches into a tale involving hot sauce in the coffee of an unsuspecting young sailor.

"We were always pulling pranks, so me and Caffy had to watch our backs for payback. Like the first time we crossed the equator."

The years disappear from Papa's face as he remembers days long gone.

"Crossing the equator for the first time is a rite of passage for sailors."

"Back in my day, us pollywogs—that's what we call those who haven't crossed the equator—had to prove ourselves. The tasks were physically challenging and often embarrassing."

Listening to Papa never gets old.

"Pollywogs have it easy today. The initiation is voluntary, more for entertainment and morale boosting."

A certificate in Papa's study commemorates his induction into the *Solemn Mysteries of the Ancient Order of the Deep*.

"The night before the crossing, the captain would go before a sailor who was designated as King Neptune and ask for his crew to be spared the horrors planned for the following day."

I join the narration, having heard the story numerous times. "Of course, the request was always denied."

"The next morning, the royal barber butchered our hair, and the ceremony began with the shellbacks spraying us pollywogs with high-pressure fire hoses. Then came the worst part—getting trash rubbed in our faces. Poor Chaffy threw up, but I managed not to vomit."

I make a face.

"Things are better today. Caffy's son got initiated after hazing got banned. He woke up to a loud ruckus, then had to crab walk to breakfast singing *Old McDonald Had a Farm*." Papa laughs. "It's probably good things have changed."

"Yes, it is." Grams joins us on the deck, wrapped in a blanket. She kisses Papa on the forehead.

The sun sparkles on the water as I listen to my grandparents share more stories. Simple moments like this make me realize how much I take for granted.

Each day really is a gift.

CJ

When Avery tells us about the bad days, I do the only thing I know to do. I draw. She needs to talk, so I'm glad I can listen, especially if Olivia is at work and can't take the time.

"Lucia doesn't understand."

Avery gives a wry laugh, acknowledging the irony. "Who knew I'd be drawn to the girl I wanted nothing to do with?"

I resist all sarcasm. Avery is hurting.

"I'm such an awful person. First, I was mean to you. And now I'm pulling away from Lucia. All I can think about is Grams and her battle with cancer."

Taking a shot would be so easy, but I'm not about to punish Avery for being vulnerable.

"You're human. Don't be so hard on yourself."

She opens up even more.

Drawing helps keep my own emotions in check, although I can tell I'm getting stronger. I can empathize without getting triggered by my own loss.

What emerges on my sketch pad is a picture of Grams on the beach. An hour later, Avery thanks me for listening.

"Anytime," I say, meaning it. I forgot how nice it is to have a friend.

On a whim, I stick my sketch in the mail.

Grams is so pleased when my letter arrives four days later; she has Papa frame my picture for her. I can't believe it. No one has ever framed my art.

"I would love to see more of your sketches," Grams tells me over the phone. "Only don't waste the postage. A picture via text is perfect."

I snap a picture of my sketch of Clementine Juliette. I'm surprised when Grams remembers the character from my mom's stories.

"Is this her?" Grams asks. "Promise me you'll draw more. You have a gift."

I feel myself redden. Grams insists I send her more sketches.

How can I refuse? The woman is fighting cancer, and she's encouraging me.

I don't know what to say.

Avery

Chemo impacts everything.

Grams started losing her hair during the second round of chemotherapy. By the third week, she's completely bald.

The hair loss was expected.

Losing her eyelashes was not.

Grams couldn't figure out why her mascara was clumping. That's when she discovered she only had four eyelashes on her lower lid.

I wanted to cry for her, but Grams just laughed at the quirky outcome. She refuses to let cancer spoil her mood.

Four weeks of chemo will be followed by six weeks of radiation. The chemo is weekly. Radiation will be daily Monday through Friday.

I document everything in what we've dubbed the cancer journal. Days 4 and 5 after each chemo treatment are always the worst, but that doesn't stop Grams.

She refuses to let treatments dictate her life, so we settle on a routine that involves ice cream, movies, thrifting and the beach.

Going to the beach is great therapy. It's our happy place after the doctor visits and treatment. A path winds through a small forest of trees at one of our local favorites.

My eyes are always scanning the shore looking for sea glass. There's just something about the search that quiets the mind. Worry takes a back seat when you're focused on finding that perfect specimen. And every piece I find just adds to the desire to find one more. There's this hope that the next find will be the rare treasure that's at the heart of the search.

We avoid the heat of the day, but still apply sunscreen. Ever since the cancer diagnosis, I don't argue about the white stuff. Skin cancer is a real threat, especially with my fair skin.

Some days Grams is too sick to walk long, but she still insists on getting out. Just sitting on a bench and listening to the waves roll in does her heart good.

Other days, we can make it for two hours before we head home for dinner.

My cooking skills have improved. Grams coaches me from the recliner while I attempt to reproduce her favorite recipes: Swedish meatballs, stuffed bell peppers with rice and ground beef, and homemade kraut runzas, to name a few.

I'm careful to include two vegetables—a fresh salad and another choice. Even when Grams can't stomach much, the doctor wants her to focus on eating small portions and drink lots of water.

She's always patient with me, even when I burn the hamburger meat or shatter a glass baking pan. At least my mess-ups aren't every day.

On Saturdays, I pack a picnic and Papa joins us. If Grams is feeling strong, we take the ferry to explore one of the beaches on Puget Sound.

I love the sound of glass clinking together in my pocket. My reward is usually a handful of small pieces, mostly in clears, greens and browns, though on a lucky day, I find my favorite teals, blues and pinks.

"What did you find?" Grams is sitting on a blanket wearing a floppy straw hat and enjoying a book. Papa tells her she looks as beautiful as ever which makes her eyes sparkle.

I open my palm, proudly displaying my find for Grams who examines each one, holding each to the light and commenting on the shape or color.

"You're getting quite the collection."

I smile, imagining the haul I'll take back in my suitcase. I might have to ship back a box because I've also found a half dozen bottles at the thrift store.

The staff knows us since we frequent the place at least once a week, sometimes two. I could buy enough glass bottles to last me a lifetime, but I put a limit on myself.

Grams is on the hunt for fun new styles to go with her head wraps, so I love browsing the racks with her. Thrifting makes the days feel normal.

Her motto: "Fight cancer in style."

Pink is her new color of choice, and a gently used pair of pink cowboy boots is now her preferred footwear. Her support group on social media loves her stylish ensembles. A pair of white overalls, a pink t-shirt, pink high-top Converse and pink headwrap is a fan favorite, gaining hundreds of likes.

Papa teases us about our thrifting obsession, but part of the hunt is to spend less than $10. There's something satisfying about getting the best deal on what turns out to be quite the treasure. As the saying goes, "One man's trash is another man's treasure."

Secretly, I think he's pleased. Grams isn't letting cancer kick her sense of style. Even the nurses are always commenting on how good my grandmother looks in her various shades of pinks and fun fabrics.

I tell her she should start a blog, but she'd rather go thrifting.

CJ

"Whatcha doing?" Amiya finds me in the treehouse and takes a seat beside me. She smells like summer—a combination of sunscreen and sweat.

I answer by showing her my latest Clementine Juliette sketch. A new sketchbook is filled with various renditions of my namesake.

"Is that the warrior princess?"

I cock my head in surprise. "How'd you know?"

"Duh?" Amiya may only be going into first grade, but she lives with teenagers. Her attitude rivals mine.

Of course, she takes the sketchbook without asking and examines every page. Amiya is full of questions. Why is Clementine Juliette crouching behind the door? Who is the image reflected in her pupils in this close-up? Does she have an animal sidekick?

My pint-sized critic even counts every freckle splattered across Clementine's nose to make sure I haven't forgotten one. When I pass the test, she praises me.

I laugh. Having a little sister is good for me.

Amiya wants to know the story behind each sketch, so I give her the abridged versions of a half-dozen. Sitting on the wooden planks surrounded by the leaves is the perfect setting for imagination to soar. I don't realize the hours have disappeared until the first fireflies blink around us, fueling my creativity.

A new Clementine Juliette story begs to be told.

Amiya is as spellbound as I was at her age.

The stories need to be told.
If only my mom recognized her own genius.

Avery

When Grams asks me to go to her monthly support group, I'm blown away by the number of people impacted by cancer. Twenty people fill the room—survivors and patients alike.

Everyone is in different stages of their journey. The survivors are there to encourage those facing the unknown. And the stories are just as unique as each individual. A stay-at-home mom of three, a businessman, a server at a high-end restaurant, a flight attendant and a kid my age.

That one really gets to me. A helmet and longboard rest against the wall behind him.

"Cool shoes." He admires my latest thrift store find, a pair of retro sandals.

"Thanks." I redden, trying not to stare at his piercing green eyes. A do-rag covers what I assume is his bald head. "Nice longboard."

When he smiles, I notice the dimple.

Grams elbows me. I know she'll tease me later.

As I listen to one of the cancer survivors talk about her radiation therapy experience, I absently play with my sea glass bracelet.

"We're quick to judge each other," she tells the audience. "But cancer has taught me one thing . . . you never know what people are carrying."

Like CJ.

I swear the speaker can see straight into my life. I regret judging CJ before giving her a chance. Honestly, I don't know what I'd do without her. When I need to get out all the crazy emotions swirling inside me, CJ listens to me for hours.

She lost both her father and her brother.

Saying goodbye to Grams will wreck me.

I take out the cancer journal and start a list. *Lessons I didn't Expect to Learn this Summer.*

1. Everyone has a story.
2. Be grateful.

Even on the hard days, I'm more appreciative than I used to be. Which seems ironic. How can facing death make you grateful?

But something has shifted in my perspective.

Tomorrow is no guarantee. Things that once consumed me no longer carry the same weight. Who posted what on social media or what people think of my outfit . . . all this deflates in the face of death.

A few months ago, I wanted nothing to do with CJ. But now the foster sister I wanted so much to hate has become a blessing I never expected. I'm grateful Amiya has CJ this summer. Because of her, my little sister is largely oblivious to everything with Grams.

When I try to thank CJ, she brushes aside my gratitude. "You would've done the same thing."

I hang up the phone, knowing the truth. I was too self-absorbed in my perfect world.

But suffering has humbled me, making me hyper aware that every day is a gift.

A gift too precious to waste.

CJ

"So, you're crushing on a guy, and you don't know his name?" It's late when Avery calls.

She reddens on the screen. "It's stupid, right? I met him at a cancer support group."

"Whoa." I wasn't expecting that. "This guy has cancer?"

She falls back on her bed and groans in response. "It's hard enough watching my grandmother suffer. I can't bear to watch someone my age face the same."

"That's tough." I turn onto my stomach and hug my pillow. Is this the same Avery I met a few months ago?

She's so pleasant, kind, empathetic . . .

And hormonal. She's got it bad for this guy.

"You should see his eyes. I've never seen that shade of green. And he's a skater."

Avery goes on for 15 minutes about a guy she spoke to for 3 minutes. The girl is clearly sleep-deprived. Caring for her grandmother is taking its toll on Avery.

I half-listen, my gaze falling on the blank canvas surrounding me. Mike and Olivia said I could paint my room, but I still can't believe they agreed to spray paint.

"Better here than on public property." Olivia laughed. "You just got off probation."

I subconsciously rub my bare ankle. Not wearing the monitor is nice.

"Create whatever you want," Mike agreed. "It's your room."

My mind has been exploding with ideas ever since.

I wonder if the ceiling is off limits. Van Gogh's *Starry Night* would be fun in purple, teal and hot pink.

"So, what should I do?"

I don't realize Avery is asking a question until she goes quiet.

"Uh, I don't know," I deadpan. "Ask for his name."

She shoots me a look on the screen. "You're not helping."

"What do you want me to say? Make out with him at the support group?"

Avery clutches her phone as if ready to chuck it at me. If we were in the same room, I can just imagine the pillow fight.

Avery

Grams' last day of chemo falls the day before the holiday, so Independence Day is not the only thing we're celebrating. I frost a cake with whipped cream and add stripes of strawberries and blueberry stars to mimic the American flag.

Papa swipes a finger through the whipped cream.

"Wait for the potluck." I threaten him with a rubber spatula.

He pouts like a kid. "Your grandmother won't let me touch her tortilla pinwheels or her bacon-wrapped jalapenos either."

"We leave in an hour, old man," Grams teases. "You won't starve."

Papa puffs out his stomach. "I have to keep my girlish figure."

I can't help but laugh.

Along with tables of food, a bounce house and a slip 'n slide are set up in a grassy area on the south side of their church. Grams can't resist the water. She doesn't care about getting her clothes wet.

Before either Papa or I can react, Grams plops on an inner tube and flies down the hill, her squeals trailing her. Several kids follow her lead.

"Your grandmother rocks," some lady tells me as she adds dish soap to the plastic slip 'n slide. Sudsy bubbles float in the air as spray from a hose hits my ankles. "I want to be just like her when I'm her age."

Sweat beads my forehead.

It is hot.

And the water is tempting.

Grams hikes back up the hill, her clothes dripping. A huge grin lights her face. "You gotta try it."

Why not? If my grandmother battling cancer can join a bunch of kids on a water slide, what's stopping me? Who cares what people think, even if I've spotted a few hot guys in the crowd?

I jump on a neon green tube and fly down the slide. The water is cold but worth the rush. Grams is right. I can't remember the last time I had so much fun.

"We should make a train." Grams corrals a group onto the slide. Stringy wet hair sticks to my cheeks as I hold onto the tube in front of me.

A little guy with freckles counts to three, and we're off. Momentum pulls us to the bottom of the slide in record time where we land in a dog pile. I'm stuck in a tangle of arms and legs.

I'm laughing when a hand reaches out.

I grasp the wrist of the faceless person rescuing me. When I start to slip, his strength pulls me to my feet. I'm staring at longboard boy—the guy from the support group.

"Uh, hey." I redden, suddenly very aware of the grass sticking to my thighs and my wet t-shirt clinging to me. I can only imagine my hair.

He's amused. "Looks like fun."

"A total blast," Grams answers. "It's Asa, right? From the support group."

When he nods, she introduces me. "Have you met my granddaughter, Avery?"

His green eyes sparkle under a trucker hat. "Nice to meet you, Avery."

My stomach growls, only adding to my embarrassment.

"I'm hungry, too," Asa saves me. "Want to get some food?"

I need a towel, but the sun will have to do—even though it's beginning to sink below the horizon. We have blankets in the car for the fireworks display. I can always use those if necessary. Fried chicken and pulled pork have my attention for the moment.

Asa has three cats, a chinchilla, a parrot and a tank of exotic fish. He wants to be a vet tech when he graduates, and he writes song lyrics on the side. He also has a dimple that shows when he smiles—something he does a lot despite the cancer.

"I know a great spot by the water to watch the fireworks," Asa says. "It's not far. I was going to take my longboard. My mom's working the night shift at the hospital."

Papa offers to drive. Grams insists on seeing the display even though she's tired.

Thirty minutes later, I find myself glancing at Asa out of the corner of my eye. There's so much I want to ask him about the cancer, about his song lyrics, about his dreams, but then he reaches for my hand, and my brain turns to mush.

Fireworks have never felt so real.

I swear my insides are exploding.

CJ

Crumpled paper litters the floor. I've been sketching for hours, trying to narrow down the ideas for my room. Mike and Olivia are serious about me painting the walls. They want me to feel at home.

I love the vibrant color of traditional graffiti, but I also love the simplicity of Banksy's style, so I've decided to combine the two. Draw the viewer into both the details and the overall effect.

Music blares from my speaker. As the notes drift in and out of my subconscious, my imagination stirs. Most of the time I don't know what will take shape on the paper. The communication between my head and my hand is mysterious—something I'll never fully understand.

Toby and my dad weave in and out of the sketches, along with treehouses and fireflies and glass bottles and waves. Clementine Juliette, the warrior princess, even makes an appearance.

When I sketch the *Starry Night* for my ceiling, I'm thinking of alternative colors like hot pink, purple and teal, but an ocean emerges in my sketchbook instead.

I shouldn't be surprised. That's often how the creative process works. I start with a vague impression, and as I create, I get lost in this place where the art takes over and my subconscious works in the background.

Obviously, our vacation to Puget Sound made an impression on me because I'm at the ocean, feeling the waves against the kayak, hearing the cry of the seagulls, feeling the breeze against my skin. Remembering the playful seals bobbing in the water beside us and feeling a peace I haven't felt in a long time.

Bubbles break the swirling lines on my sketch. Instead of the sky, I'll stare up at the sea, my mind tumbling in the waves as I tumble off to sleep.

A glass bottle comes next. Against the clean white page, I imagine this as a large stencil, the image taking up a third of one wall.

My imagination is on overdrive.

I may not emerge from my room for weeks.

Avery

"Want to get matching tattoos?" Grams is in the kitchen, wearing yoga pants and sipping a cup of hot tea.

I stumble into a bar stool, half asleep. "Am I dreaming?"

She grins. "Your parents already agreed."

My eyes bug out. "You're serious?"

"As long as the tattoo is small and discreet." Her eyes twinkle. "Nothing too crazy."

I can't believe it.

"I start radiation therapy next week." Grams takes a seat beside me. "Remember what the radiation therapist told me?"

"About getting a couple of small tattoos?"

She nods. "To mark the spots where I'll get my treatment."

I have the notes written in the cancer journal. Apparently marking the area for treatment helps with accuracy.

"I figure if I have to get tattooed for cancer, why not get something I want?"

I can't help but smile at the unexpected conversation. Papa is covered in ink. Grams' milky skin is flawless except for the age spots on her hands.

We spend the next hour discussing different designs and whether to go with the pink cancer ribbon or something symbolic. On a whim, I search for sea glass tattoos and scroll through various designs before something catches my attention.

"Oh, look at this." I show Grams my screen where pieces of different shaped sea glass form a heart.

A smile lights her face. "Yes, that's the one."

I'm impressed with the shading. The artist has captured the play of light on the surface of the glass with incredible detail.

"Do you like the blues in this design?" Grams finishes her tea as we consider our options.

"What about shades of pink?"

"To symbolize cancer," Grams finishes my thought.

We waver between the ankle or collarbone. The collarbone would be closer to the area impacted by cancer, but I've always liked ankle tattoos.

"Let's go with the ankle." Grams picks up her phone. "Walking along the shore, the waves circling our ankles in our search for sea glass—it's just fitting."

"You're really serious?"

Her face glows. "Why not?"

She pulls up the number for a local tattoo shop. In seconds, Grams is talking with the tattoo artist.

We have appointments in two days.

CJ

The text must be a prank.
Or maybe a bucket list thing.
I reread the words again.
Can you design me a sea glass tattoo?
A picture pops up.
Something like the one in the picture?

My dad was the tattoo artist. Not me. I'm too critical of my work. A tattoo is something permanent. Not easily erased.

The pressure is too much.
But who can say no to Grams?

Avery

Asa thinks getting a tattoo is cool.

I'm focused on the pain.

We've been talking since the fireworks, so he's trying to convince me I'm not a chicken. "You're braver than you realize."

So why do I feel like I could puke?

My nerves have been on overdrive since we walked into the tattoo shop an hour ago. But if Grams can go through cancer treatment, I can deal with my fear of needles.

I've been known to pass out any time I get a shot.

"It stings a little, but it's not bad." My grandmother shows off her ink. "And it looks great."

I try to ignore the pink tinge to her skin and take a seat while the tattoo artist tells me about giving his grandmother her first tattoo.

"These boomer divas are some of my biggest clients." He sterilizes my skin with rubbing alcohol. "One chick in her 80's is getting two full sleeves—a field of wildflowers on the right and an aquarium on her left."

I hope Grams doesn't get any ideas. My heart thumps in my chest anticipating just one small tattoo. And I'm feeling queasy.

"Smile." She takes a picture.

Grams has the tattoo artist laughing with all her stories as a Navy wife. She's trying to distract me which is good. The needle stings.

I take deep breaths, forcing myself not to faint.

"You got one cool grandma." The artist smiles at me. "Maybe I'll see if my Nana will get a matching tattoo with me."

Somehow, I make it without losing consciousness. I even manage to relax halfway through the process.

An hour later, my artwork is done.

Grams is right. My eyes trace the outline of each piece of glass. CJ did an amazing job with the design. The shapes are so unique and the shading perfect.

It's beautiful.

CJ

"Your artwork looks amazing." Grams shows off her tattoo when we video chat after the appointment. "I love it. Thank you, CJ."

It's so surreal to see what I created on a canvas of flesh.

Olivia's eyes water. She'll cry when we get off the phone. Seeing her mother get thinner and paler with each call is hard even though Grams rocks the head wrap.

"Look at mine." Avery points the camera at her ankle. "I'm glad I braved the needle."

Even the critic in me can admit the tattoos look good. I wonder what my dad would think.

"I want a tattoo." Amiya squeals, pleading with her parents. "Please pretty please with lots of whipped cream and a cherry on top."

"I don't think so." Mike laughs. "I still can't believe one of my little girls has a tattoo."

The irony isn't lost on me.

The girl who hated me now has a permanent reminder inked on her skin.

Avery

Grams has been lathering herself with lotion, but that doesn't alleviate the itching or the burning that comes with the start of radiation therapy. One of the people in the support group suggests a cream with calendula and rose hips. After four days, the burns have faded into a tan.

When I record the results in the cancer journal, Grams sees the page I added.

"Lessons I didn't Expect to Learn this Summer," she leans over and reads. "What's this?"

"Just some random thoughts." I shrug. "The cancer survivor who spoke at the support group got me thinking."

"Me, too." Grams gazes out over the ocean in front of us. We're sitting on one of our favorite benches, taking in the beauty. Off to our right, a chocolate Labrador and his owner play fetch with a piece of driftwood.

"Add this one to your list," Grams says after several minutes. "We were never meant to carry our burdens alone."

She leans against me as I write. "Have I told you lately how glad I am that you're here?"

I don't trust myself to speak, so I just squeeze her hand and listen as the waves roll into shore.

"Forgive and let go," Grams breaks the silence. "That's a big one. Don't waste precious seconds complaining and hating."

I'm still writing when Grams starts laughing, a deep belly laugh that makes her shoulders shake. I love that cancer hasn't taken her sense of fun.

"Let me guess." I scrawl out the next point. "Laugh every day."

"That's a good one." She wipes her eyes. "But I was thinking about a speech I heard years ago at a military ball."

My mind sees a framed photograph on the fireplace mantel. The one of Grams and Papa all dressed up. He's wearing his dress uniform while Grams wears a floor-length red gown. She looks stunning.

"One of the admirals talked about the importance of making your bed every day."

I narrow my eyes. Not the speech I would expect at a military ball.

"My thoughts exactly." Grams reads my mind. "The speaker quoted a retired Navy four-star admiral who wrote a book called *Make Your Bed: Little Things That Can Change Your Life . . . And Maybe the World*.

I give a humph.

"According to the author, making your bed begins your morning with a small success that will encourage many more throughout the day."

I wiggle my toes in the sand, processing the idea.

"So, my takeaway from cancer is this." Grams taps on the journal. "Get up, make your bed and get dressed everyday—no matter how you feel."

I stare out at the water, considering the theory.

Lounging in my pjs is nice on lazy days, but seeing Grams out of bed and dressed in her fun pink clothing combinations makes the day open with possibilities.

Who knew making your bed came with mental health benefits?

Maybe it's being intentional about the little things that make a difference in the big things.

CJ

My closet is so stuffed, I can't open the doors without a shoe or sketchbook escaping. The room is bare except for the furniture. I keep waiting for Mike or Olivia to come down the hallway, saying they changed their minds.

What other foster parent would agree to the whims of my creativity? But Olivia is the one who took me shopping to get the spray paint. She even convinced me to buy sheets of Mylar for my stencils. The medium weight is better than my makeshift cardboard boxes and easy to cut with a utility knife.

Plastic sheeting covers the floor, as well as the bed and dresser. As I cover the mirror, I admire the bucket hat and denim overalls I found at the thrift store. Grams has inspired the whole family to upcycle.

"Will you let me see your masterpiece as the walls progress?" she asked the last time we talked.

I would say no, but that hardly seems fair to a woman battling cancer.

Lola wanders around the empty room, sniffing at bottles of spray paint. A half dozen life-sized Mylar stencils line the walls. My window is open for ventilation, and the ceiling fan whirs above me.

I'm already on a creative high; I don't think the spray paint will make a difference.

Avery

Even though the nurses prepare you for the side effects of radiation (fatigue, skin reactions, nausea and dry mouth), it's still tough seeing Grams suffer.

The loss of appetite is the worst. Grams is even smaller than before, a wispy thing just under a hundred pounds. Her weight terrifies me.

I've been trying new recipes, foods with lots of spices to draw out the flavor—anything to help Grams eat. But she can only stomach a few bites.

Going to the beach becomes less frequent. Most days we curl up on the couch watching movies before she drifts off to sleep, or I'll read to her. Psalm 23 brings her much comfort.

> *The Lord is my shepherd, I lack nothing. He makes me lie down in green pastures, he leads me beside quiet waters, he refreshes my soul. He guides me along the right paths for his name's sake. Even though I walk through the darkest valley, I will fear no evil, for you are with me . . . Surely your goodness and love will follow me all the days of my life, and I will dwell in the house of the Lord forever.*

I wish I had the same faith, but I'm afraid.

"You're quiet." Grams wraps herself tighter in her blanket. We're sitting on the deck after supper, the breeze off the Sound cooling the evening air.

"I'm just tired," I say. Who wants to talk about dying with someone facing death?

But Grams knows what I'm avoiding. "It's okay to talk about death. I'm not afraid of dying."

Tears spring to my eyes. I've resisted the subject for a reason. I can't bear the thought of losing Grams.

"This life is just the beginning."

I don't voice the doubts that fill my head. How can she be so confident? So sure?

"Faith is believing what we can't see." Grams reads my mind. "Like the wind. You can't see it, but you see the effect, the evidence."

My gaze falls on the hanging plants. The fuchsia petals shimmer in the breeze as Grams settles back in the wicker chair. How can she be at peace when I'm such a wreck?

"I'm not a betting person," she says after several minutes. "But if Jesus is the only one who came back from the dead, eternal life seems too big a gamble to go with anything else. If I'm wrong, what do I lose?"

Tires crunch against the winding gravel driveway. Papa is back from the store.

"I don't have all the answers." Grams touches my hand before I help unload the groceries. "But God is pleased even with faith the size of a mustard seed."

I head down the stairs, remembering a recent recipe that called for mustard seed. I was surprised to find a small container in the spice rack.

Before moving in with Grams and Papa over the summer, my cooking skills were limited to preparing hot dogs and mac and cheese. I barely used ground pepper. Mustard seed didn't even cross my cooking vocabulary.

Talk about tiny seeds.

Each one is maybe 1-3 millimeters in diameter, so if my mental math is right, somewhere around 2,500 mustard seeds fit in a single teaspoon.

Maybe I could get behind a faith that small.

CJ

The ceiling is complete. Now I can start on the walls. Olivia and Mike can't wait to see the final masterpiece, but I make them swear not to peek before the reveal.

Grams has been my biggest cheerleader. She loves every picture I send her, responding with dozens of heart emojis. In seconds, she calls to video chat.

"You finished the ceiling?"

Grams leans into the screen in anticipation. Her breath catches as I trail the phone the length of the entire picture.

"CJ, that's incredible. Like Van Gogh's *Starry Night*."

"You get my inspiration?" My voice rises in excitement above the doubt.

"Of course," Grams exclaims. "The swirls and colors are so similar, and yet you've managed to make the sky an ocean. It's brilliant."

I don't know what to say. My inner critic has been screaming all day.

"Your parents will be impressed, too."

My parents?

At first, I'm confused. My dad's gone and my mom won't visit me at my foster home.

But then I realize Grams means Mike and Olivia. She senses my hesitation because she adds, "I understand the guilt. It took me awhile before I could call my in-laws Mom and Dad."

A lump forms in my throat.

"It's okay to love Olivia and Mike. You're not betraying your parents. Our hearts just expand."

How does Grams know I've been struggling with guilt?

Pushing people away before they hurt me is my norm, but Mike and Olivia don't quit. They continue to stick by me.

When they hung a large family picture from our trip to Puget Sound in the living room, I fled outside before my emotions tumbled out in a snotty mess.

The hardest part of being in foster care is walking by all the family pictures hung on the wall and not seeing a single picture of you.

And yet, there I was in the picture, sandwiched between Avery and Amiya, surrounded by Mike and Olivia, Grams and Papa as we smiled for the camera.

I look so happy.

And yet a tear slips down my cheek at the thought.

The walls around my heart are crumbling.

And that terrifies me.

Avery

I wake up with a start, surprised that it's almost noon. Grams had a rough night, so we were up until the early hours of the morning.

Papa must be at the American Legion with his buddies. His truck isn't in the driveway. He admitted that he wouldn't leave the house if I weren't here, so I'm glad he gets a break.

I don't hear Grams, so I pad across the wooden floor in my oversized t-shirt. My skin prickles when I push open the bedroom door.

Grams is so pale, but she's breathing.
Barely.

I run for my phone and fumble with the keypad. My hands shake as I call 9-1-1.

I forget I'm still in my pajamas until I see my reflection in the hallway mirror. Worry lines my face. I throw on shorts and a t-shirt. A ball cap is quicker than a brush.

Ten minutes later, the EMTs load Grams onto a stretcher. A head scarf adds a splash of color to the blanket draped over her frail frame. If Grams were fully conscious, she would be happy I covered her head. An oxygen mask engulfs her face.

I want to ride in the ambulance, but that's not an option.

"Sorry, kid," the EMT with the dreadlocks says. "Can you call an Uber?"

"I've already called my grandfather," I manage to choke out. "He's on his way."

Grams disappears inside the ambulance. Before the door closes, I flash the sign for, "I love you."

I almost lose it as the vehicle pulls out of the driveway.

The siren screams down the street, its mournful sound echoing the pain pounding my heart.

CJ

I almost fall off the ladder when Amiya startles me. I'm engrossed in the tree taking shape on the wall with the window.

She holds a sandwich on a plate. It's not the first time I've forgotten to eat.

"Mom said no starving artists in her house."

I climb down from my perch. Paint speckles my sleeves.

"You look like a painting." Amiya laughs at me as I inhale the food, not realizing how hungry I am.

"Thanks," I say through a mouthful. Manners are trumped by food.

Amiya steps closer to the wall to examine the branches woven around the window frame. Besides Grams, she's the only other person who has witnessed the transformation.

"I'll use stencils for the leaves," I explain to my little art lover.

Last week Amiya slipped into the room while I worked on the ceiling. I don't know how long she'd been there when I finally noticed her presence. The girl lay on the plastic, arms under her head, oblivious to wet paint splatter. The look on her face was priceless—she was completely mesmerized by the colors and swirls of the ocean taking shape above her.

At night, I do the same. The reading lamp casts a soft glow on the walls as I lay on my bed and stare at the artwork. My eyes trace over every line, taking in the details that merge into pictures.

Usually, I get lost in the design until sleep overcomes me, but last night my imagination was on overdrive, so I traced my latest idea on a piece of Mylar.

Banksy's stencil idea is brilliant. I just hope the idea in my head translates to the wall.

That's the thing about creating.

Sometimes you just never know exactly how something will turn out.

Avery

Papa nearly collides with a car when he speeds through an intersection on a red light. He's not thinking straight. Grams is his world.

When we arrive at the hospital, he barges through the door like a tornado ready to destroy anyone in his path. "My wife? Where is she?"

The nurse at the emergency desk tells him the doctor will give an update as soon as possible.

He paces back and forth like a caged animal until I lead him to a quiet spot in the corner. Papa collapses on the seat and buries his head in his hands.

"I should've been home." He pulls at his hair. "What kind of husband am I?"

"A good one." I pat his arm. "Grams doesn't want you trapped inside all day. It's not good for either one of you."

Wild eyes look at me. "What am I going to do without her?"

Seeing him so helpless is a punch in the gut. Papa has always been my rock.

I don't know what to say. The same fear haunts me. *What am I going to do without Grams?*

So, I say nothing. Just reach out my hand and touch his wrist.

"We've been married 42 years. That's over half my lifetime."

Papa is lost in memory, his mind pulling up pictures he shares with me from the past.

Grams on their wedding day in a simple white dress and daisies woven in cascading long hair.

The birth of my mother and my uncle.

Countless moves with the military and opportunities to travel the world.

"Your grandmother is a strong one." Papa sighs. "When I had to be out to sea, she was always thinking about the other wives and organizing fun outings for them and the kids. It wasn't easy being separated for months at a time, but I never heard one complaint from her lips."

I'm so lost in the stories, I almost forget we're in the hospital. Everything comes rushing back when the doctor approaches. His look is grim.

Papa jumps to his feet. "Is she going to be okay, Doc?"

The question hangs in the air, the awful space between the knowing and the unknowing.

The doctor shakes his head. "I'm so sorry."

Papa drops to his knees. The cry from his mouth knives my heart.

I blink, sure that I didn't hear the doctor right.

The doctor says more.

Something about a weakened heart, but I can't process the words.

Time slows or speeds up. I'm not sure which.

My mind is a vacuum, all thought suspended.

This must be what they call shock.

Sounds of people talking and the television swirl around me. The smell of coffee combines with disinfectant in a nearby mop bucket. A wave of nausea hits.

I grab onto a chair before I hit the ground. I force myself to be strong. Papa needs me.

And I need him.

Grams can't be gone.

CJ

The sound of shattered ceramic brings me running. Olivia stands in the kitchen, broken pieces of her favorite mug at her feet. Coffee pools on the wooden floorboards.

I know the pained look on her face.

It's the same look my mother had when she got the awful news of the accident.

Avery is crying on the phone.

Grams is dead.

Avery

Someone uses a badge to open the emergency room doors, and we follow in silence. I stare at my feet, my mind registering the squeak of my tennis shoes on the linoleum.

The hospital staff gives us privacy.

My grandmother rests on the hospital bed.

Too still.

"Grams?" My voice wavers as I touch the hand resting atop the covers.

Her flesh is so pale. Strangely stiff. Everything in me wants to deny the facts, but my tears reflect what my heart already knows.

She's gone.

My sweet grandmother is dead.

"No."

The lone word escapes my lips as I collapse into a hospital chair. I'm not ready to let go.

Grams can't be gone.

She was supposed to beat the cancer. She has another 10 or 15 years. What about my graduation? Summer vacations on Puget Sound? My wedding day?

Papa leans over the hospital bed, cradling Grams in his arms.

His mournful wail pierces my heart. The sobs racking him are painful, raw.

When our eyes meet, he doesn't see me. He's too lost in the heartache. A fresh wave of grief hits me hard, taking my breath away.

As much as my own heart hurts, I can't bear to see him suffer. What will Papa do without Grams? They've been best friends and lovers for over four decades.

I leave quietly, giving him space to say his goodbyes.

I don't speak when I call my mom.

The silence says everything.

Neither of us can bear to talk, so we hang up, promising to connect later.

Papa emerges from the hospital room an hour later, and we drive home in silence.

He disappears to the bedroom, so I leave a note on the kitchen counter. I doubt Papa will notice my absence, but I don't want to add worry to his grief.

I need to escape.

There's an old bike in the shed. The back tire is flat, but an air pump works magic. My heart thumps as I pedal like a mad woman.

I'm on autopilot.

The beach is the only place that will bring any comfort.

Ten miles separate me from my destination. Good thing I remembered to bring a water bottle.

I'm drenched in sweat, but the sound of the waves rolling into shore speaks to my soul like music.

I leave the bike against a pile of driftwood and step out of my tennis shoes. Several people dot the shore, looking for shells or playing with their dogs.

How can life go on when my world stopped? Did anyone feel the atmosphere shift when Grams took her last breath?

Her absence heightens every sense.

The sound of the gulls, their cries echoing my own.
The taste of salt water in the air.
Sunlight sparkling on the waves.
The sand between my toes.
The cool water against my ankles, my tattoo covered in sea foam.

I walk along the shore, my eyes absently drawn to the sand as memories float around me.

Coffee and ice cream dates.
Conversations about everything and nothing.
Searching thrift store bins for buried treasure.
Our frequent beach trips during her treatment.
Grams and me looking for sea glass.

I'm staring at a beautiful rose-colored piece of glass shaped like a heart before my mind registers what I see. I wonder how many other pieces I've missed, lost in my thoughts.

I bend to retrieve the glass and rub the frosted glass. Grams would be cheering at such a find.

I swallow the lump in my throat. I close my fingers around the piece.

This one will be made into a necklace.

A glass heart resting near my heart, a daily reminder of my grandmother.

CJ

Olivia is busy with funeral arrangements, so I call my caseworker to tell her the news.

"You'll need respite," Jillian says. "Do you know when they plan to fly to Washington for the funeral?"

"Saturday, I think."

"Okay, I'll reach out to a few people. Ms. Sherita just got the call for twin babies, so she's a little busy to take in a teenager for a week or two. Mom was an addict, so the babies are going through withdrawals."

I hate respite, but Ms. Sherita has a big heart. The woman has fostered over 70 youth in the last 30 years. Last time she provided respite, Ms. Sherita gave me a hug when I left. The gesture was unexpected. I usually feel like a burden. An inconvenience.

"I want to go," I blurt out.

"Go where? To the funeral?"

My announcement surprises Jillian. Turnover is common with caseworkers, but Jillian's been with me almost the whole time. Some kids in the system go through a dozen or more caseworkers. But Jillian is my second. She just graduated from college, so I'm one of her first cases. "Are you sure that's a good idea? I don't want you getting triggered."

I let out a deep breath, pushing down the panic. It's a bad idea, but I want to do this for Grams. Even though I've only known her for a few months, she's always treated me like her own granddaughter.

Then there's Avery.

She needs me.

Someone who knows loss.

A friend who can be present with her in the pain.

"I'll be fine."

I must sound more confident than I feel because Jillian doesn't ask any more questions.

Good thing she can't see the tremor in my hands. They haven't stopped shaking since we started talking.

I tell Jillian goodbye, hoping I'm not making a huge mistake.

Going to another funeral will bring back every painful memory I've tried to forget for the last three years.

Avery

I force myself to be strong for Papa. Mom needs help with arrangements, and he's hurting too much to focus. Since Grams died, he just sits on the deck and stares out across the water.

Lost.

I count down the time until my parents arrive. Forty-eight hours, and their flight lands. I've never been more desperate to see them. I just want a hug.

Navy friends and people from the church bring food. Lots of food.

Too much food.

Neither one of us has an appetite, and I've run out of storage. The refrigerator and freezer are full of casseroles.

But I don't know what to say when the doorbell rings with another person handing me a foil pan. They care about my grandparents, and I'm grateful for their support. Papa needs friends more than ever.

So, I plaster on a smile and say thank you like my mother told me to do.

I'm just a kid.

I have no idea what I'm supposed to do. The whole thing is so overwhelming, I want to break down in tears.

I want my mom.

CJ

"Does it ever go away?" Avery searches my face. "The pain?"

I meet her gaze, knowing that look that dulls the pupils. The same eyes stare back at me when I look into the mirror.

She's waiting for me to reassure her, but the loss of someone you love never truly leaves. "It doesn't sting as much, but there's always a dull ache."

Avery gives a small nod. "So, my heart won't always feel this way? Like I can't breathe because of the pressure?"

"Time helps, but there are always rough days. Things that trigger the pain."

The silence should be awkward, but there's something about suffering that breaks down walls. Avery's not the same girl I met when I moved in with her family. She might've tried to empathize with my loss, but the head and heart understand things completely differently.

"I hate black," she finally speaks, frowning at her dress.

"I hate dresses."

The smallest smile crosses Avery's lips.

I'm glad Olivia didn't make me wear dress shoes. My black high-top Converse feel more comfortable.

Avery's eyes well with tears. "I don't think I can do this."

We're sitting in a corner at Grams and Papa's church waiting for the funeral to start. The last 48 hours are a blur. I barely remember the flight. I still can't believe we're back in Washington. If only the circumstances were like before—a vacation and not a funeral.

Avery looks so lost.

Enduring all the condolences is rough. I still remember all the awkward words, the number of stiff hugs after the accident.

"I got you." I reach for Avery's hand and squeeze cold flesh. I remember how much I wanted someone to sit with me, the simple presence of another human reminding me I wasn't alone.

"Thanks." She mouths, not able to talk.

"Ready?"

Avery shakes her head.

"We could always run." My teasing works. I get a snort of laughter.

"And have the police show up?"

"Yeah, probably not a good idea."

She looks so miserable; I hate feeling so helpless.

The whole thing brings back memories I keep trying to stuff, but I haven't had a panic attack—which is good. Just a queasy stomach.

Ever since we arrived, I sense a difference. Like my heartache has made me extra aware of Avery's pain. I haven't been able to see out of my own pit for three years, so empathy is good.

My therapist would be proud. I guess I'm listening to her more than I realized.

The preacher seems young, but he's known Grams and Papa for almost 20 years. He opens a small notebook and reads a list of lessons Grams wanted to share. Apparently, it was Avery's idea to keep a cancer journal with notes from the doctors, food to eat and what to avoid, along with other helpful information. The lessons are gems sprinkled throughout the journal.

I find myself leaning forward in the pew, curious.

"*Lessons I didn't Expect to Learn this Summer* by Avery and Grams," the preacher begins.

Sniffles echo in the sanctuary.

"Everyone has a story. Be grateful. Lean on each other. We were never meant to carry our burdens alone."

Olivia wipes her eyes, and Mike puts his arms around her. I might've been jaded about foster care until I met them. But leaning on them has been a blessing.

"Get up, make your bed and get dressed everyday—no matter how you feel."

That one gets a few laughs from the audience.

"Forgive and let go. Don't waste precious seconds complaining and hating."

"Aren't these great?" The pastor looks over the audience, and several people make noises of agreement.

"Laugh every day."

Tears slip down Avery's face, so I scoot closer to her so there's no space between us.

Her eyes register gratitude.

Bringing her comfort is a gift I didn't expect.

Maybe I'm finally starting to heal.

Avery

Papa and I sit on the deck long after the others have gone to sleep. A petal from Grams' fuchsia falls from the flower basket into my lap like a pink tear. I finger the soft petal and look over at my grandfather.

"I can't convince you to come with us?"

He shakes his head. "Not now."

Moving away from his friends would be too big a loss after saying goodbye to Grams, so my parents are finding someone who can help with meals and grocery shopping.

I wish school didn't start in two weeks. Otherwise, I'd volunteer to stay with Papa longer.

"Take her collection of sea glass," Papa tells me. "She would want that."

I can only nod as a fresh wave of emotion hits.

Sea glass will forever remind me of Grams.

CJ

Mike books a red-eye flight for the trip home, so we arrive sometime in the early morning hours before the world wakes up. Between lack of sleep and the funeral, the next few days blur before me. Grief has left us all reeling.

I can't sleep.

Or paint.

I'm completely numb.

I sit coma-like on my plastic-covered bed, unable to move. Grams was a fighter. She was supposed to beat the cancer.

A knock registers in my subconscious. Amiya is at the door wearing an oversized Hello Kitty shirt that hangs to her knees. Her hair is matted on one side while the other sticks out. Puffy eyes meet mine.

"You can't sleep either?"

She shakes her head.

"Come here." I pull her into a hug, my chin touching the top of her head. This is one of the things I miss the most about Toby—having the chance to be his big sister.

"Can we paint?"

I let go, and Amiya steps back. Long eyelashes frame the question in her eyes.

Her request is so unexpected, I take a moment to answer. "Paint? Like on a canvas?"

Maybe I'm having one of those waking dreams. But I squeeze my fingers into a fist and feel a fingernail bite my flesh. I'm not dreaming.

Amiya points to the mural taking shape around us. Two walls are still blank. "Can I help you paint the walls?"

I glance at my phone. It's 2:38 in the morning. I hesitate, knowing Olivia would want her daughter to be asleep.

"Please," Amiya pleads. "You can paint over it."

I let out a long breath.

She doesn't know what she's asking.

I haven't painted since we got the news about Grams. After Dad and Toby died, I couldn't create for months. The guilt was too much. I was alive, and they were gone. How could I do something I loved when they weren't coming back?

My therapist finally convinced me to honor the dead by living. But still the familiar guilt hits. Grams had so much life to live.

"Pretty please," Amiya says again, breaking my thoughts.

I take a deep breath. For whatever reason Amiya needs this. Maybe I do, too.

"I guess."

Amiya chooses her favorite color and pushes the trigger on the spray paint like a woman on a mission. The girl knows what she wants.

She wields the can like a weapon. As Amiya sprays the wall, her body contorts with emotion. The sway of her hips. The flash of her hand. Her posture. Anger, hurt, pain, sadness—it's all written in her body language.

Purple explodes across the wall. Color taking on the language of pain and heartache.

I grab a can of hot pink and join Amiya. We go at it like a pair of crazed artists. Bold streaks, zigzags, splashes—our arms are a flash of motion.

Avery joins us at some point. I'm vaguely aware of her beside me, a can in each hand. The girl doesn't waste any time.

Something about firing the paint is cathartic. A relief. Like the splatter brings the messy emotions out in the open. There's freedom in not hiding or stuffing what we don't know how to process.

When the cans run out, we don't hesitate. Amiya grabs Carolina blue, I choose cornflower yellow, and Avery goes for orange.

A deep guttural sound escapes Avery's lips as we cover every square of white in color. Amiya is next, her groans echoing her sister's pain. Something bubbles inside me, and I find myself letting out a whoop. Soon the three of us completely lose it—we're whooping and laughing and crying all at once.

Feet rush down the hall and the door swings open. Olivia arrives first with Mike on her heels.

"What's wrong?" she blurts out as her eyes widen, taking in the scene.

We stop abruptly, suddenly jarred out of our creative space. The present comes rushing back with the full force of a speeding train screeching to a stop. I can almost see the sparks from the friction.

"Uh . . ." I'm the first to speak, though nothing intelligible comes out of my mouth. I feel like a criminal.

The can slips from Amiya's hand and hits the plastic covering the floor. Specks of paint dot her face like freckles. "I'm sorry. It was my idea."

"No, it was me." Avery is not about to let her little sister take the blame.

Neither Olivia nor Mike speak. They both stare at the wall, their mouths slightly open. I turn my head, seeing the entire picture for the first time. The mix of colors looks like a palette of paint got overturned, bleeding over the entire wall. The effect is mesmerizing. Like something unleashed.

"I don't know what to say. It's . . . it's . . . incredible." Olivia turns in a circle, taking in the whole wall. "It's like you brought color to every emotion that I'm feeling."

She's right. There's anger and shock and hurt and pain and sadness and joy all jumbled together, splattered on the wall, screaming to be seen.

Acknowledged.

A six-year-old figured out what I've taken years to conclude.

The pain I tried to stuff came out in other ways.

Unhealthy ways.

The feelings too awful to process can't be hidden.

They need to come out for healing to begin.

That's why Amiya needed to paint.

And why Avery grabbed two cans.

What was inside begged to be released.

As I stare at how the paint swirls together in what seems like chaos, there's raw beauty in the mess.

Vulnerability.

We don't always know what to do with the ugly feelings. The helplessness. The anger. The emptiness.

But feelings don't need to be rational.

Or explained.

They need to be felt.

We feel because we're human.

Avery

My stomach growls. My parents went to bed an hour ago, but we're too wired to fall asleep.

The three of us sit on the plastic-covered floor staring at the explosion of paint around us. Empty spray cans litter the floor. I feel like a kid imagining shapes in the clouds.

"That looks like a tornado." Amiya points to a patch near the window that funnels upward.

"Do you see the cat chasing the mouse?" CJ eyes a section halfway down the wall.

I cock my head. No wonder she's the artist. My imagination is lacking. All I see is a semi-circle and two small lopsided triangles.

She traces the air, too tired to move. "That's the face with the ears, and there's the mouse running toward that hole in the corner."

I shake my head. "Still not seeing it."

"Right there." Amiya jumps up and outlines the supposed creatures, then claps her hands in delight. "Don't you see it?"

Maybe we're delirious from spray paint fumes because we bust out simultaneously with laughter. Soon we're all howling like crazy people. Snorting and giggling at silly things.

The paint splattering our skin like freckles.

A dust bunny floating in the air.

The grumble of our stomachs.

Amiya disappears and returns with a bag of Doritos and a pack of Oreos. We devour every last crumb.

I imagine Grams sitting beside us enjoying the fun. She would've grabbed a can of spray paint and jumped right into the fray, laughing with us, and licking the frosting off an Oreo.

A flood of warmth rushes over me.

My grandmother would be pleased.

I've been in a funk since her death, but I can almost hear Grams whisper.

Don't stop living. Each moment is a gift.

CJ
Christmas
Four Months Later

I stare out the front window for the tenth time, my breath frosting the glass. The ground is covered in fresh snow. It's cold, but the roads are clear. She shouldn't be late.

"Can we wait five more minutes?" I can't hide the disappointment in my own voice. I wanted this Christmas to be different.

"Of course," Olivia agrees, but I can see the doubt in her eyes. The smell of baked bread and ham fill the air. Everyone is hungry. I feel bad for making them wait.

Maybe inviting her to Mike and Olivia's house was a bad idea. Will my mom feel like she's competing with another family? She sounded excited to join us for Christmas dinner, but maybe she was just pretending for me. Otherwise, Mom would've shown up by now.

The white lights on the Christmas tree cast a soft glow in the room. Lola is playing with a forgotten piece of wrapping paper, evidence of the presents we opened an hour ago.

My name is stitched across the top of a stocking. A penguin wearing a striped scarf smiles back. This is my third Christmas in foster care, and it's the first time I've had my own stocking.

I tell myself not to cry. My mom stopped celebrating holidays and birthdays after the accident. The reminder of happier times was too much.

"I'm sorry, kiddo." Papa gets up from the recliner and ruffles my hair. We picked him up from the airport yesterday. "I know you miss her."

I give him a hug because I don't trust myself to speak. This is Papa's first Christmas without Grams. Even in his pain, he's still worried about me.

We head to the dining room when the screech of tires makes my head spin. I swing open the door, and a blast of air bites my flesh. An old VW van with faded pink and orange flowers careens into the driveway, just missing the mailbox. My mom jumps out of the passenger side wearing a long overcoat and black boots, a plastic container in her hand. The driver has dreadlocks—someone I don't recognize.

"Am I late?" She calls to me, out of breath. "I've been trying to find a ride all morning. I didn't want to miss out on dinner."

Olivia joins me at the door, hugging herself to keep warm. "Merry Christmas. We were just gathering around the table."

My mom waves off the driver.

"Your friend can join us." Mike comes to the door, still wearing a Santa hat.

"He's not my friend." Mom steps inside and gasps, her gaze taking in the Christmas decorations and furnishings. "I hitched a ride."

If Mike and Olivia are shocked, they keep a straight face. Instead, they welcome my mom like she's royalty. Mike takes her coat and Olivia offers her a pair of slippers.

"I brought your favorite." My mom pushes the container toward me like a peace offering. "Chocolate chip cookies."

"Thanks." I swallow the lump in my throat. They're store-bought, not like Grams' homemade cookies, but I'm still impressed. My mom is trying.

"What a beautiful piece of jewelry." Olivia notices the silver necklace with the birthstones on Mom's neck.

Her eyes dart toward me, and I see the panic, but she recovers. "It, uh, it was a gift from my husband."

I let out the breath I'm holding.

"Something smells delicious." Mom changes the subject. "Thank you for inviting me."

I thread my fingers through hers as we follow Olivia to the dining room.

I wonder what Mom thinks of the family pictures hanging on the wall. There's a collage of vacation photos and an impromptu shot of the family at the pumpkin patch. Even my school photo hangs next to Avery and Amiya's pictures.

It's so strange having my mom as a guest in the home where I live. We sit side by side at the table, our first Christmas together since the accident.

When Papa introduces himself, I realize my mom has never met the people I've known for over six months. Other than a few pictures I've shown her on my phone, she knows little of my life here.

Amiya snags a crescent roll, but Mike stops her midbite. She's wearing a knitted hat I gave her.

"Let's bow our heads," he reminds her to pray. "We have a lot to be grateful for."

I open one eye during the prayer, half-afraid my mom will disappear. Her hands are pressed together, lips slightly parted as she listens. My mom isn't a mirage. She's here sitting next to me wearing a holiday dress and a sprig of holly in her long hair.

I was worried things would be awkward. But there's not one dull moment between Amiya's antics and Mike and Papa's bad jokes. Laughter and conversation swirl around the room like the aromas from our feast.

I can't stop staring at my mom. Dad always called her his pretty princess, but even then, she was completely unaware of her natural beauty.

I want to memorize every moment.

Her bright eyes.

Mike's toast to family.

Amiya's hiccups from the sparkling grape juice.

A dollop of whipped cream on Mom's lips from the pumpkin pie I helped Avery make.

I don't want the moment to end.

Even Papa seems to enjoy himself, though I catch him getting a far-off look once or twice, and I know he's thinking of Grams.

The same thing happens to me when I think of my dad and Toby. I will always hold their memories close to my heart.

"So, we have a tradition," Mike interrupts my thoughts. "Have you ever heard of the game *Aggravation*?"

My mom claps. "We used to play that all the time when I was a kid."

I had no idea.

When Amiya disappears to get the handmade board, Mike explains the marble game. I guess it's kind of like the board game *Sorry*, but apparently, more aggravating.

Two rounds later, both teams tied, we launch into the tiebreaker game. Me, Mom and Papa against Mike, Olivia and the girls.

The stakes are high. The losing team cleans dishes. Olivia brought out Grams' China plates which means no dishwasher.

Even Lola gets excited. She's sitting on Avery's lap, barking every time someone gets knocked off.

My heart pounds in my chest when I roll the dice. Mike and I are in a race to home base.

I groan when I get a four. I needed a three.

Mike blows on the dice, drawing out the suspense.

"Go already." I roll my eyes. He knows I don't like to lose.

The dice clatters on the table, stopping on a five.

"Yes!" Mike pumps his fists, and his team cheers as he takes his marble home. Amiya jumps up and dances around the table with Lola on her heels.

"I guess we have dishes, kid," Mom admits our defeat.

Papa offers to dry the dishes, but we insist that he take a nap. I won't admit it, but I'm secretly happy for the loss.

Washing dishes together with my mom sounds like a win to me.

Avery

I excuse myself when Asa calls to video chat. He wants to know if Santa's elves brought me a special gift.

"Thank you." I show off the sea glass ornament he mailed me. The glass pieces catch the light, making the colors dance like light hitting a prism. "I'm going to keep it out year-round. It's too pretty to be packed away."

Of course, he wants to see my collection, so I give him the abbreviated version of the contents inside every bottle on my shelf. Where I found the glass, how long I've had it, the stories Grams and I made up.

"I'm probably boring you." I redden when I notice the time.

Asa shakes his head. "I find it fascinating. This whole trash turned to treasure idea has captivated me since you showed me your bracelet."

I subconsciously clutch the necklace Mom and Dad gave me for Christmas. The pendant is made from the heart-shaped sea glass I found the day Grams died.

Asa whistles. "That's beautiful."

We talk another 30 minutes before my mom calls me to join the pajama party. It's tradition to dress up in our flannels and watch *A Christmas Story*. My dad is obsessed with the movie. Last year, we got him a leg lamp as a gag gift.

"I almost forgot," Asa says before we say goodbye. "I got the best Christmas gift ever."

I hold my breath. Asa had an appointment two days ago, but he hasn't said a word about what the doctor reported. "Did you get good news?"

A grin breaks across his face, stretching from ear to ear. "I'm in remission. The cancer's gone."

I give out a loud whoop.

I couldn't be more thrilled.

CJ
Six months later
June

Family meetings are still strange for me, but I like how Mike and Olivia give their daughters a voice.

Better than being invisible.

Like the foster care system makes me feel.

Lola presses her nose against my knee wanting to be pet. Maybe she senses something. Dogs are in tune to things humans may not recognize.

Which makes me a little nervous.

Why exactly did Mike call a family meeting?

Is it Papa? He tries to be strong, but every time Olivia calls to check on her father, I hear the loneliness in his voice.

Mike tents his fingers together. "Papa has decided to sell the house."

"No." Amiya bursts into tears. "You can't sell Grams' house."

Avery pales, but she doesn't speak.

"But there's good news," Olivia is quick to add. "Once the house sells, Papa is going to move in with us. He loved being here at Christmas."

Amiya's tears turn to cheers.

"The change will be hard for Papa," Mike says. "But it will be good for him to be with family."

He will be the grandfather who will be in the bleachers, never missing a sporting event or school concert. Snapping pictures of his granddaughters to send to his Navy buddies. Maybe Papa will even go to the mall if one of my paintings gets selected to be featured in the multi-school art show.

But just as suddenly as the thought enters my head, fear slams me in the gut. *If Papa moves in, does that mean I move out?*

"What do you guys think?" Mike leans forward in his chair. "Wouldn't it be great to have Papa around all the time?"

Amiya jumps up and down with Lola on her heels. "Papa can sleep in my bedroom. We can get a bunkbed, and I'll take the top. It will be like a sleepover every night."

Mike and Olivia laugh.

My own heart sinks. I shouldn't be surprised. Just when I start to get used to my new foster family, the bottom falls out.

I want to disappear but that's one of the rules for family meetings. Everyone participates.

An animated discussion follows. Will Papa sell the furniture? Who will help him pack? Will we road trip across the country in a small moving truck?"

Mike notices I'm quiet. "Are you okay?"

What am I supposed to say? I have no say in my life.

"You and Avery will have to share a room until I can finish the basement."

"You want me to stay?"

"Of course." Mike throws a decorative couch pillow at me. "You should know that by now."

Now Avery is the quiet one.

I stare at my feet, knowing the answer.

No way will she agree to room together.

Later when I can't sleep, I climb into the treehouse, wondering if I could live among the branches until Mike finishes a room in the basement. I wouldn't need much. A mattress, a pillow, and my comforter.

Laying back on the wooden planks, I peer through the opening in the ceiling. If we avoid winter, maybe I can convince Mike and Olivia.

The idea of falling asleep under a blanket of stars makes me sleepy, so I close my eyes. The faint smell from the neighbor's fire pit drifts on the air while cicadas hum around me like white noise.

I don't realize I've fallen asleep until I hear the creak on the stairs. Avery's head pops through the opening in the floor.

"Sorry." I'm quick to sit up. "I'll give you your space."

"It's okay. I couldn't sleep."

I prop myself up, leaning against the wall. Maybe sharing a room for the summer won't be so bad. Every day will come with ups and downs, but we did survive the loft together last summer when we vacationed on Puget Sound.

Avery sits across from me, legs crisscrossed.

"It's so weird to think of someone else living in my grandparents' house. If I was older, I'd buy it."

I know the feeling. A year after I got put in foster care, I was in my old neighborhood when a family parked in our driveway and walked inside the house. Mom couldn't keep up with the payments, but the white house with the window boxes still felt like home.

I keep thinking about our handprints in the concrete Dad poured for the shed out back and the marks on my parents' doorway, showing our growth each year. Toby would stretch out his arms, trying to be as tall as me. The memory brings a smile to my lips.

What would I do without these little snapshots of my past? Every time I recall something, Toby and my dad feel extra close.

"Tell me your best memories," I say when Avery falls silent.

Soon she's lost in the past as memories float around us, filling the treehouse with the sweetness of remembering.

I can almost feel Grams wrapping us in a big hug.

Avery
Two weeks later

Papa's house sells in a week, so the plan is to get one-way flights and rent a small U-Haul truck for the trip home. That way we can help him move across the country in combination with our annual summer vacation.

Grams loved Whidbey Island, so Papa rents an Airbnb at Oak Harbor in honor of her. The island in Puget Sound is one of her favorites, but we've never been, so I'm excited for the new adventure.

Our noses are pressed to the window when we drive over the bridge at Deception Pass. The view of the narrow passage takes my breath away.

We stop to walk across what is actually two connecting bridges before we hike through the old growth forest to the water below. Papa is content to wait on a bench while we explore.

"Don't mind me." He waves us off. "I've been here a dozen times with Grams."

I look back once to see him sitting there alone and feel the familiar twinge of loss. Grams has been gone almost a year, but her absence will always be with him. Being together with someone over four decades, intertwines two souls.

Amiya freezes halfway across the bridge, so I hold her hand. Even though there's a pedestrian walkway, cars and trucks rumble past us, a little too close for comfort.

CJ peers over the edge and whistles. "That's a long way down."

"About 180 feet," Dad says.

Amiya's fingernails dig into my flesh, distracting me from the breathtaking view.

"You got this." I tell Amiya, wanting to linger more, but not wanting to make my little sister suffer. The poor girl is ash white.

She doesn't let go of my hand until we step off the bridge. Then her pent-up fear gushes out in a torrent of words.

"ThatwassoscaryIalmostcriedmyheartfeltlikeitcouldexplodeinmychestcanwegodowntothewaternow?"

I can't help but laugh as we hike down the path through the old trees towering above us. I inhale the earthy smell as I take in the ferns and moss and twisted roots and limbs which envelope us.

"I need my sketchbook." CJ walks behind me, equally in awe.

We round the last bend of the trail, the sound of water calling me. Waves roll onto a stretch of sandy beach dotted with driftwood. My happy place awaits.

"Picture time." Mom points to a boulder to the right. The bridge forms a picture-perfect backdrop.

CJ is the first to crest the top while I help Amiya.

"Beautiful." Mom snaps the picture.

"Do you want me to take a family picture?" A woman walking a Labrador offers, so Dad and Mom join us on the boulder.

Of course, we also take a goofy shot complete with bunny ears and silly faces.

"That one's going in the annual Christmas letter," Mom announces.

CJ pulls out her phone. "I can take one of the four of you."

"Not a chance." Mom gives her a hug. "You're part of the family. Cheesy vacation pictures, ugly Christmas sweaters and all."

Emotions roll across CJ's eyes like the waves at our feet. Gratitude. Acceptance. Peace.

"Look up there." Dad points to an eagle's nest.

As if on cue, an eagle soars across Deception Pass. Talk about impressive.

"Now, I need a sketchbook."

CJ snorts. "Maybe you could take a picture instead."

She's right. I'm not an artist.

But that doesn't stop me from chasing after her. The water is cold.

Perfect for a good dunking.

CJ

"This little town was one of Grams' favorite places on the planet," Papa says over lunch at a hamburger place called Toby's Tavern in Coupeville. "You'll love it."

Above the bar hangs a carved wooden sign which shares the *probable* history of the bar which came by square-rigged ship around Cape Horn, arriving after 1900, and surviving both Prohibition and a fire.

If only the walls could talk, as they say.

I can just imagine the stories.

An hour disappears when Mike says he has a surprise. He rented kayaks for us to explore Penn Cove.

No one expects my excitement.

Amiya is the first to see the starfish in the low tide waters around the pier. The colorful creatures are everywhere, so I snap a picture. I want to capture this in my sketchbook later.

"Did everyone sign the waiver?" Our guide hands out life jackets. We're the only ones signed up, so we get a private tour.

Avery and I share a tandem kayak the color of candy corn.

"Don't tip." She pushes off the pier with her oar and wobbles the kayak.

"Don't get wet." I splash her, feeling more confident than a year ago. Avery isn't the only one who's changed since we first met.

The mountains are to our backs as we pull ahead of the others. I'm excited to see the baby seals the guide told us about. Apparently, seals love to sunbathe and snooze on the rafts used to harvest mussels.

"Mussels are good eatin'." The guide smiles. "And mussel farming provides a habitat for many species. Each adult mussel filters roughly 15 gallons of water a day. This makes for a healthy marine ecosystem."

"Sounds like a great school report," Mike eyes me and Avery.

No thank you. Summer vacation just started.

Water laps against the sides of the kayak as we quickly find our rhythm. I inhale the fresh air, grateful to be included in another family vacation. I'm falling in love with the Pacific Northwest.

We hear a sound like a cross between a baby human and a kitten followed by a splash as we approach the first raft, a small wooden dock anchored in the water.

"There's a baby and his mama." Our guide says in a low voice, pointing his oar toward the right. "They heard us approach, so they splashed into the water."

A small grey head peers above the water next to a bigger head. I don't know who's watching who. Us or them.

"He's so cute!" Amiya squeals in the kayak with Mike, forgetting to be quiet.

"Look," CJ points to another seal in our wake.

I pull out my phone to record the seals. They don't seem agitated by our presence—just curious.

Avery and I break away from the others and circle around several rafts, careful to be as quiet as possible. Most of the seals splash into the water before we can get a good picture, but finally we approach a large female who doesn't leave her spot on the mussel raft. She blinks at us, continuing to sun herself without moving. Apparently, she's unconcerned by our presence even though we're only separated by a few feet.

"This is so amazing," I whisper.

Other heads bob in the water around us. I can't believe the number of seals.

We near another raft when Avery gasps, making me turn. Four babies are sunning on the platform, their little faces adorable. I control the urge to squeal in delight.

I seriously need to pinch myself. I know our time is almost up, but I don't want this moment to end. Talk about bucket list experiences. I will be sketching for days to capture every detail.

I snap another dozen photos before the guide says we need to head back to the pier. He has another group of kayakers waiting for a tour.

Thirty minutes later, Papa treats us to gelato at an Italian place. The frozen treat threatens to drip on my phone, but our heads are pressed together around the screen watching the video footage.

Papa smiles. He didn't join us because kayaking is too much on his back, but he has similar memories with Grams.

One moment is extra sweet.

Papa tells us how he'd just returned from six months out to sea.

"I missed Olivia's sixth birthday, so we went to Whidbey Island and celebrated with gelato." A smile lights Papa's face. "My daughter may be 37, but it feels like yesterday."

Papa tweaks Amiya's nose, and she giggles.

"I can still see Olivia and her brother enjoying the treat like we are today. Grams was snuggled into the crook of my arm, happy that I was back on land. She never complained about my time away. She focused on the time we had together and treasured every moment."

I make a mental note to sketch this moment for Papa.

It's the least I can do for the man who treats me like another granddaughter.

Avery

I've been dreading this moment, even though I know this is what Grams wanted. She chose to be cremated so her ashes could be scattered over the water.

The smell of coffee drifts from the kitchen at our Airbnb, but Papa isn't sitting at the bar stool. From the window, I make out a lone figure on the hammock overlooking Oak Harbor.

I'm guessing he didn't sleep much, so I grab a throw blanket. Yesterday afternoon, I spent an hour in the same place scanning the water with a pair of binoculars, hoping to spot a whale.

The faint smell of oregano reaches my nose as I walk past two raised planter boxes of herbs and approach the hammock.

"You're cold." I wrap the blanket around Papa's arms. "How long have you been out here?"

He shrugs.

It's too dark to see the water below. "We should go if we're going to make sunrise."

Papa says nothing as he follows me back to the house like a lost puppy. Everyone is in my grandparents' Highlander, though CJ and Amiya are half asleep.

Mom and I crawl in the back beside them while my dad drives toward the shore. Papa stares out the window cradling a velvet pouch.

Dad parks and we head the short distance to the beach. A seagull soars above us. No one talks, everyone lost in thought. We leave tomorrow, so Papa thought sunrise would be the best time to say our final goodbyes to Grams.

Sleep mats my eyes as we walk toward the water. I kick off my flip flops to feel the cool sand between my toes. The sun is just peeking above the water in the east, coloring the sky with the first streaks of pink and orange.

A tear slides down my cheek. Grams is everywhere.

The briny smell of salt water on the slight breeze.

The roar of the waves crashing onto shore.

The cry of a seagull looking for food.

We huddle together staring at the wisps of pink and splashes of yellow and orange unfolding before us. Grams would've been equally mesmerized at the beauty.

"She loved the ocean," Papa breaks the silence. "Every duty assignment with the Navy was a chance to collect shells and sea glass at a different beach. Okinawa, Japan, Norfolk, Virginia, Coronado Island, California . . . she loved the ocean."

My gaze follows the debris left behind with the retreating tide, but no sea glass catches my eye.

Everyone says a few words in honor of Grams—even CJ. When all eyes look at me, words fail me. I can only tell Grams how much I love her before I dissolve into tears.

"It's okay." Mom pulls me close. "She knows."

Papa walks out into the waves, and we follow. Amiya carries a bouquet of wildflowers, so she hands us each a flower. I drop a daisy onto the surface, admiring the beauty of the petals floating on the water.

Papa opens the velvet pouch and says a prayer before overturning the contents. The wind picks up the ashes and spreads them over the water. In seconds, a wave swallows them under the surface and carries them out into the deep.

"Goodbye," I whisper, my words lost in the crash of waves.

Everyone heads back for shore, but I'm not ready to leave. I'm not wearing a swimsuit, but that doesn't stop me from diving under the water. My t-shirt balloons around me as I let the waves embrace me.

My tears mix with the salt water.

CJ

I grab a purple Sharpie marker and help Amiya decorate a large welcome sign in polka dots. The girl knows what she wants. Lots of color and bold letters to welcome Papa home.

Amiya wants to surprise him, so the girls left the hotel early this morning in the Highlander—two hours before Mike and Papa rolled out in the U-Haul.

Of course, Amiya can't escape the marker which gets on her face and arms. At least she's wearing a paint shirt. I've convinced her of the merits of protecting her clothes.

"Looks like you need help to hang your sign," Avery walks into the room in a pair of denim overall shorts she found when we went thrifting. Grams would be thrilled. We go at least once or twice a month—turns out thrifting is a good way to bond.

We fasten the sign to the pillars out front minutes before we hear the honking. Mike backs into the driveway in the small truck. Papa doesn't have a lot. He gave Grams' clothes to a women's shelter and sold most of the furniture.

"Help us unload these boxes," Mike calls out to our crew. "Then I'm ordering pizza."

Amiya claps, getting Lola excited. The dog weaves around our legs, trying to figure out what's happening.

I still can't believe Avery agreed to give up her room, but the girl is full of surprises. We spent two days emptying her room before we left for Whidbey

Island. Avery insisted it would be better for her to move so I could keep the room with the mural.

Amiya asked if I would paint over our explosion of color, but I love impressionism and street art, so the result is perfect. In true Banksy style, I added several stenciled designs in white. A message in a bottle, Clementine Juliette, warrior princess, and a little boy holding a toy dinosaur. The contrast makes the images pop. I couldn't be happier.

I just hope Avery doesn't change her mind.

Tonight, we test the new room arrangement.

Fingers crossed we survive.

Papa is exhausted, so Olivia forces him to sit down while we unload the truck.

"So, that's how it's going to be, huh?" He laughs when his daughter hands him a glass of lemonade. "You moved me here so you could boss me around?"

"Yep." Olivia nods. "You better get used to it."

Papa watches the parade of movers walk past him with boxes, clearly enjoying the attention.

Lola licks Papa's fingers, no doubt remembering the man who spoiled her at Christmas with the dog treats he keeps in his pocket. He pulls out a small biscuit for her which she finishes in seconds.

Papa isn't the only one getting pampered.

Lola is going to be more spoiled than ever.

Avery

A year ago, I would've staged a protest.
Or circulated a petition.
Anything to argue my rights.
Giving up my room to sleep in a twin bed next to my foster sister would never have been an option.
But I guess even my stubborn self can change.
Plus, I would do anything for my grandfather. I'm so glad Papa agreed to move in with us so he's not alone.
Sleeping in a different space is an adjustment. There's no room in the closet, so my winter clothes are stuffed in bins in the garage. And it's super tight with two beds, but at least CJ doesn't snore.
So, I'm willing to make the sacrifice.
Grams would be pleased.
Papa needs us, and family sacrifices.
I just wish I could fall asleep, but my body is not cooperating. The clock taunts me. I've been tossing and turning for over an hour. Tomorrow will be brutal. I'm babysitting for a family with three kids over the summer. I need sleep.
Lying here, surrounded by color and images, I feel like I'm immersed in the middle of a painting. I'm mesmerized by the white stenciled silhouettes highlighted by the night light, especially the one of the little boy holding the toy dinosaur.
Toby.
CJ's little brother.

"You up?" She whispers, sitting up in the bed across from me.

I don't tease her about the night light even though I prefer a pitch-black room. CJ can't do the dark. Constantly changing foster homes doesn't exactly make a person feel safe.

So, even though I won't admit it, I'm proud of my parents for sticking this foster thing out. CJ's mom has had more good days than bad since Christmas, so there's hope for reunification. But in the meantime, we're here for CJ—no matter how long the process takes.

"Sorry you had to give up your room."

I shrug. "You did, too."

"At least you don't pee the bed like my last foster sister."

"That's disgusting." I make a face. I'm already dreading changing diapers all summer.

We spend the next hour talking about her stenciled designs. CJ tells me all about Banksy, a graffiti artist who inspired her. I'm impressed.

The stenciled leaves framing the window highlight my treehouse in the backyard while Clementine Juliette leaps off the wall. The warrior princess definitely needs her own book series. When I ask about the message in the bottle, I'm surprised to learn about the bottle CJ tossed overboard the ferry last summer. I had no idea.

"I know it's silly," she says. "But I figured if you could find sea glass, maybe I could find a real message."

I raise my eyebrows. "Did you?"

CJ shakes her head. "But when I started researching, I learned about a mom who wrote a message to the son she'd lost, and it inspired me to do the same."

Something Grams once said comes to mind.

We're all kind of like sea glass. If you give CJ a chance, you might discover a story you never imagined.

I would be a hot mess if half my family died. Losing my grandmother has made me painfully aware of the hurt in others. I'm ashamed I was so quick to judge CJ when we first met.

"Something inside me shifted that day," CJ admits. "I've been so angry since the accident, but releasing the bottle brought closure."

A yawn escapes my mouth. My eyes are glazing over, so maybe I'm imagining things on the ceiling above me.

"Are there three hearts in that swirling wave?"

CJ nods. "For my dad and Toby and Grams."

Only the most observant would see the camouflaged hearts.

"It's my way of remembering them before I go to sleep each night. A small tribute to their lives."

I never thought I would relate to the foster girl I hated so much. CJ and I are so different, and yet the common threads of loss, grief and pain touch every life.

"I wish I had more time to get to know her," CJ breaks my thoughts. "Grams made me feel like family."

Family.

The word hits me.

I would've never gotten through the last several months without CJ. Her support has meant the world.

"Thank you."

"For what?" CJ knits her eyebrows.

"For listening to me." I meet her gaze. "For being present even when I didn't know how much I needed you."

She nods slowly. "Turns out, I needed you guys, too."

I reach out between the twin beds to give CJ a hug and misjudge the distance in the shadows. I lose my balance and fall onto the floor. CJ collapses in a fit of laughter.

"So much for a touching moment," I snort as I return to my bed, all dignity gone. "I was trying to be genuine."

CJ laughs harder.

"You're just as annoying as my little sister."

"Annoying?" CJ throws a pillow at me. "Look who's talking."

I duck, and we both fall back on our beds howling.

"I think it's official," I finally catch my breath.

CJ cocks her head. "What's official?"

"Annoying sisters mean we're really family."

Sneak Peek: *Headlock*

Prologue
Late August 2018

He hates himself for getting caught.

His lawyer pulls paperwork from a briefcase. The power suit does little to ease his fears. The guy is too busy for small talk.

The clock shows five minutes before the hour. His parents sit behind him. His mother scans the room for anyone she might know. His father gives a curt nod to his colleague, lips pursed together in a tight frown. He's not used to being on this side of the courtroom.

All rise when the judge opens the side door.

He loosens his tie. The ugly thing strangles him, making him even more uneasy.

The judge looks like he could make a drill sergeant wet his pants. His black coat stretches over broad shoulders as he looks out over the audience, his eyes narrowing over a hook nose. The judge is one of two juvenile judges for the county with a reputation for his no-nonsense approach to criminal activity.

His knees buckle.

"Take a seat," the judge bellows from his bench, then spits out a long monologue about rights.

The clock ticks on the wall, the second hand taunting him.

Tick, tick, tick.

He wants nothing more than to run out of the courtroom. But where would he go? Cops patrol the halls. They'd tackle him in minutes.

Tick, tick, tick.

Every little movement is heightened as if playing out in slow motion. From the corner of his eye, he can see his mother straighten the pleats on her skirt. Her perfectly manicured nails tremble. His father clears his throat, obviously uncomfortable at the lack of control.

Even his lawyer straightens a stack of papers.

Not a good sign.

The power suit may talk a good game, but even the best lawyers lose cases.

He wants to bury his head in his hands, but he forces himself to remain seated, back and shoulders straight, eyes focused ahead.

There is no jury. Just the judge.

"I'm going to give it to you straight, son. I'm dismissing the drug charge, but the assault is inexcusable. A life of privilege comes with responsibilities. Bottom line: you're spoiled. Two weeks in juvenile detention will make you think about your choices."

He blinks, trying to process the words. The lawyers reached a plea bargain. His lawyer said the judge would likely follow the recommendation. That he'd get probation at most.

But the tears in his mother's eyes and the look of disdain from his father confirm his nightmare. His lawyer mutters a few curse words under his breath, no doubt angrier about losing the case than his sentence to juvie.

He resists the urge to punch the table.

How will he survive two weeks behind bars?

Skyler
SEVEN WEEKS EARLIER
Sunday: Almost midnight
Early July 2018

I've spent most of my 13 years in a headlock.

That's life when you're stuck in a family with all boys. Poor Mom. Even Greco and Roman, our two Labrador retrievers are males. (Yes, they're named after the style of wrestling that prohibits holds below the waist.)

I'm the third son in the lineup: Jax, Gator, me and Petey. We breathe sweat, testosterone, and too much Axe body spray. Throw in a couple jockstraps, and my very existence is a daily wrestling match.

So, I should be able to escape this predicament without a problem. But wiggling out of my brothers' grasp is one thing. A wrestling injury left Jax with a weak left wrist, and Gator has a ticklish spot at his collarbone. They used to gang up on me, but I got smart, anticipating their moves and foiling their strategy. After years of practice, I can escape their grasp in under half a minute. Five seconds on a record day.

But this current unfortunate quandary doesn't involve a pair of arms locked around my neck. It's sometime near midnight in a pitch-black cabin in the woods. Somewhere between the stages of sleep, my subconscious registers a door open and footsteps pad across the wooden floor. I feel someone hover over me, but my eyes are too thick with exhaustion.

Something inches alongside my sleeping bag, its weight pressing against my side. My brain fights to put the pieces together, but I'm too groggy to move.

Scaly cold skin touches my flesh, jolting me with a start. I'm fully awake, all senses on heightened alert and heart thudding in my chest.

My insides scream, but I don't make a sound.

I'm in a headlock with a snake.

The hiss of a forked tongue sends a shiver down my spine. A thick snake slithers around my neck. I'm guessing the thing is at least four feet long, but the room is too dark for me to determine length, or more importantly—whether the snake is venomous.

I'm a self-proclaimed outdoor enthusiast. Snakes and spiders and other critters don't usually bother me, but even I don't want to sleep with something I can't see. Better to leave the big guy under a rock.

Of course, the culprit who left behind my reptilian friend is long gone. The cabin door swings open on its hinges. I know exactly who to blame.

Berkley is going down for this stunt. The guy's a dead man. I'm already calculating how to shave his eyebrows or sabotage one of his meals. When I'm done, he won't know what hit him.

I'm guessing the snake is a bull snake since they're common around camp. Bull snakes aren't poisonous, but they will bite if provoked. Of course, I could be totally wrong. The cabin is dark after all.

If the snake sinks its fangs into my neck, I can't panic. That's Rule #1. Staying calm slows the spread of venom throughout the bloodstream. Rule #2: Don't suck out the poison. More than one person has died this way.

I try not to dwell on the possibility of death. I turn 14 in a month. I barely have any facial hair.

I don't hear an ominous rattle, but if this bad boy is a rattlesnake, I'll have nightmares for years. I almost crapped my pants once when I stumbled on a rattler sunning itself on a rock.

The threat is enough to give me doubts. Berkley knows better than to mess with a rattler, but our rivalry runs deep. And he's just mean enough to choose something that will leave a mark.

Sweat beads my forehead as I remember what we learned in Boy Scouts. Apparently, more people die each year being crushed from vending machines than snake bites, but that does little to comfort me now.

The creature presses its weight against my skin, closing my airway.

I can't breathe.

Death by snake: not the epitaph I want on my tombstone.

My brain fires a message to my paralyzed muscles: *Move!*

It's now or never. I close my eyes, praying it's only a bull snake and jump to my feet. The door is next to my bunk, a mere 15 feet away. I hustle outside. Thankfully, the sudden motion is enough to send the snake flying off my neck as I rush out the door. The creature is momentarily stunned. For a brief second, we gape at one another as if waiting for the other to move. The moonlight illuminates creamy scales and dark blotches. I'm staring at a bull snake.

Good thing I'm not in any real danger. My brothers are no help at all. I could be writhing on the ground, foaming at the mouth, and they'd still be sound asleep. Their snores drift through the open door. No one stirs because we stayed up too late playing pool in the game room. I'd be dead before Jax or Gator came to my rescue. But I can't blame them; it was a long day of cleaning the cabins, getting ready for the next round of campers.

The bull snake slithers off the porch and into the trees. Seeing the thing stretch to full length makes me shudder. The reptile is over five feet long. If only I'd gotten a picture, proof of my escapade.

A burst of laughter over my shoulder breaks the silence like a gunshot. I scan the woods for Berkley. A pair of menacing gold eyes pierce the darkness, but they probably belong to a predator—not my nemesis. Of course, Berkley doesn't have the balls to reveal himself.

If only the jerk went home with the other campers. Most kids come to camp for a week, but Berkley's parents pay for a month of babysitting. I think they would opt for the whole summer, but even my dad, the camp director, has his limits with the spoiled brat.

"Very funny, Berkley," I call into the darkness. "Watch your back. I'm coming after you when you least expect it."

Berkley just howls as if mimicking some primeval call of the wild. Even the coyotes don't respond, the cry too pathetic to answer.

"Laugh now." I clench my fists, my mind filling with sweet possibilities of retaliation. "You won't be amused when I get my revenge. This is war."

> Download your free e-copy at:
> www.angelawelchprusia.com

A Note from the Author

Are you obsessed with sea glass now like me? I would love to see your unique finds. Contact me at www.angelawelchprusia.com to share your pictures and be the first to know when new books come out.

Thank you for reading *Sea Glass Stories*. Your reviews and word of mouth are the best compliment I can receive for one of my books, so please tell your friends. I would love to connect. Follow or message me:

Instagram @angelawelchprusia
TikTok @angelawelchprusia
Facebook @angelawelchprusiaauthor
www.goodreads.com/author/Angela_Welch_Prusia

Acknowledgments

Soli Deo Gloria. For God's glory alone.

Will. I love doing life with you. Your support is invaluable.

Blake, Sheila, Leo, London, Meghan, Keely, Dad, Mom, Amy and Brian, Sarah and Andrew, Benjamin and Nancy, Will and Patsy, Kim and Darrol, Tammy and Dennis, and all of my nieces and nephews. My life is richer because of each of you.

Cover designer, Mercedes Piñera. Your design stood out from the beginning. Thank you!

My talented beta readers and editors from around the globe: Julia Cusick, Adah Davis, Jennifer Melham, Christy Wissink, Caroline Kohls, Kinsey Kaiser, Raynbow Corleone, Kathy Tulley, Ariana Oprea, Sofia La Fata-Hornillos, Eve Anstey, Funmi Oyedokun and Abigail Nunez. Your feedback has made this story so much stronger. Thank you, thank you, thank you.

And finally, my readers. I'm so grateful you joined me for a story close to my heart.

Made in United States
North Haven, CT
15 September 2025

72876776R00176